The
Peverel Papers

The Peverel Papers
Flora Thompson

A YEARBOOK
OF THE COUNTRYSIDE

With illustrations by C.F. Tunnicliffe

Edited and introduced by
Julian Shuckburgh

Century
London · Melbourne · Auckland · Johannesburg

First published in 1986 by
Century Hutchinson Ltd
Brookmount House, 62-65 Chandos Place
Covent Garden, London WC2N 4NW

Century Hutchinson Publishing Group (Australia) Pty Ltd
16-22 Church Street, Hawthorn, Melbourne, Victoria 3122

Century Hutchinson Group (NZ) Ltd
32-34 View Road, PO Box 40-086, Glenfield, Auckland 10

Century Hutchinson Group (SA) Pty Ltd
PO Box 337, Bergvlei 2012, South Africa

Designed and produced by
Shuckburgh Reynolds Ltd
289 Westbourne Grove, London W11 2QA

Design: David Fordham
Design Assistant: Carol McCleeve

Typeset by SX Composing Ltd, Rayleigh, Essex
Printed in Portugal by Printer Portuguesa

British Library Cataloguing in Publication Data
Thompson, Flora
    The Peverel papers: a yearbook of the
    countryside.
    1. Country life——England——Hampshire
    2. Hampshire——Social life and customs
    I. Title   II. Shuckburgh, Julian
    942.2'7082'0924   DA670.H2

ISBN 0-7126-1296-3

Contents

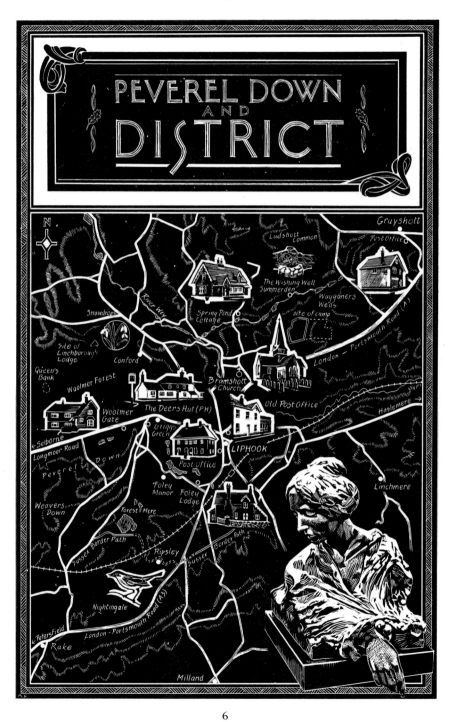

Introduction

*F*LORA THOMPSON wrote these notes on nature and country life for a weekly magazine called the *Catholic Fireside* between 1922 and 1927, when she was in her forties. She was then living in the small town of Liphook in Hampshire, where her husband John Thompson was postmaster; and she continued to write them until he was transferred in 1928 to Dartmouth in Devon and she and the family moved with him. Although they contain fictional elements, and many place-names are disguised, these notes are nevertheless a precise description of the landscape and natural history of the Liphook area. They are Flora Thompson's first large-scale prose writings, published fifteen years before she began *Lark Rise*; and already, as in her later works, she is concealing names and places and events, and to some extent her own personality.

These concealments, once we unravel them, reveal something not only about Flora Thompson's life and character but about the development of her literary technique. What we know of her life as a whole is almost entirely derived from her own writings, and since these writings all contain fictional elements their reliability is by no means clear. The semi-fictional style familiar to all readers of *Lark Rise to Candleford* was invented and developed fifteen years earlier in *The Peverel Papers*; and by examining how it evolved we get a clearer view of Flora Thompson's work as a whole.

Flora was born on 5 December 1876, the eldest child of Albert and Emma

Timms, in the tiny Oxfordshire hamlet of Juniper Hill. She went to school in the neighbouring village of Cottisford, and left home for the first time at the age of fourteen to work a few miles away as a clerk at Fringford post office. After four years she left Fringford, took a number of short holiday-relief engagements in rural post offices in various parts of the country, and then applied for and landed the job of assistant at Grayshott post office in Hampshire. There in due course she met her future husband, himself a post-office clerk. When in 1903 he was transferred to the main post office in Bournemouth, they were married and began life together in this large seaside town. Flora was then twenty-six.

The Thompsons remained in Bournemouth for fourteen years, during which their two elder children, Winifred and Basil, were born. In 1916 they moved to Liphook, and a younger son, Peter, was born a year later. For twelve years they lived in Liphook, until another and final posting for John Thompson took them to Dartmouth in 1928, where they remained until his retirement in 1940. Flora Thompson died on 21 May 1947, and was buried in Dartmouth.

This bare outline of events can be filled in to some extent from Flora Thompson's own writings. In *Lark Rise to Candleford* and *Still Glides the Stream* we are given a vivid account of what must have been on the whole a fulfilling, if restricted, childhood. At an early age Flora acquired a taste for reading, perhaps encouraged by her mother and later by an uncle, which was thought quite abnormal by her contemporaries, and positively disreputable by her husband and his family. In *Heatherley,* which describes Flora's three years at Grayshott at the turn of the century, several of her lifelong interests can be seen taking shape: the longing for education and culture and to become a writer; the sharply critical eye for petit-bourgeois pretension; and the passions for solitary walking and for the study of nature. But we must remember that all of these books were written in the last decade of Flora's life. They are recollections with the full benefit of hindsight, and largely suppress the agony of yearning for what might have been.* On many matters they contain a consistent viewpoint – such as the fundamental question of the values of rural society as she had known them in her youth, and the extent to which these values had been undermined by the march of "progress". These late works,

---

*The account in *Heatherley* of Flora's friendship with "Richard Brownlow" gives a broad hint that she felt the fates could have been kinder to her, but only because it makes no mention of John Thompson. In the circumstances she could hardly have made the matter clearer. There is also a passage in the last chapter of *Candleford Green* in which the narrow outlook of the Thompson family is described.

despite the name-changes and minor disguises, are remarkable for their clear-eyed honesty. Flora's vision of rural life half a century earlier is un-romanticised. The grinding poverty is not concealed, and its consequences are described in detail. So when Flora Thompson concludes that, in the break-down of the old rural order, more has been lost than gained, we are persuaded to believe her.

From the writings of her early middle age, however, a much more confused – and from a biographical point of view a much more revealing – picture emerges. *The Peverel Papers* are ostensibly a series of "nature notes", presumably commissioned as such by the *Catholic Fireside* magazine in which they appeared. They do indeed contain a great deal of observant natural history, botany and country lore, and a detailed description of the landscape of south-eastern Hampshire. But in addition they reveal something deeply sad and attractive about their author: she had no confidence in her own personality, and felt obliged to invent a fictitious Flora Thompson, worthy of being the author of these papers.

The process took place in two stages. In 1920, Flora persuaded the editor of the *Catholic Fireside,* who had already accepted several of her short stories, to publish a monthly column entitled "Out of Doors in January" and succeeding months. "January" was well-received, "February" was longer, and by "March" the articles were filling an entire page of the magazine. In them the authoress describes herself living in a cottage in the New Forest (although some place-names are actually in the Liphook area) accompanied only by her dog Boojie; she is visited by a young actress friend called Fiona from London, or by "Father Conlan from Boldrewood" (presumably Boldre, near Lymington); and in her long, low-ceilinged parlour: "I have gathered together my books and pictures, the old writing table at which my father wrote out his prescriptions, my grandmother's blue and white china, and the samplers of my great-aunts." Her time is spent walking, reading, writing, making jam and baking cakes for visitors. On one occasion in July, Father Conlan is bringing "his friend and former pupil, the Poet, to be introduced to me". In October, "I am already making my winter plans. I have taken down my Dante, and placed it with the Italian dictionary upon the little table by the hearth". This idyllic, if rather precious, style of life must have represented an unfulfilled dream for Flora; she had already been in Liphook, and away from Bournemouth and the New Forest, for nearly four years by the time she wrote in these terms. She was in fact living in the cramped quarters next to the post office in Liphook,* with three children to look after, and working behind the counter every day with her husband.

---

*Now the premises of the Midland Bank.

The readers of the *Catholic Fireside,* however, seemed to like her work, for she was invited to continue in 1922. But she now decided upon a change. The articles were rechristened "The Peverel Papers", and the scene was quite different – no longer the New Forest, but a cottage, "a mere snail-shell of a place . . . tucked away amongst pine and holly at the foot of the Peverel Downs". This was the downland around Liphook, where she had lived for three years before her marriage, and in which she was to remain for the next six.

There is no Peverel near Liphook, and it is unclear why Flora Thompson decided on a pseudonym,* or indeed how the name occurred to her in the first place. It has an ancient Norman origin, and this may have appealed to her romantic sense of the antiquity of the place. On the Isle of Purbeck, visible from Bournemouth where she had lived for sixteen years, there is a Peveril Point just beyond Swanage. Or a little further west there is Bradford Peverell, near Dorchester, which may also have caught her antiquarian attention. Whatever its source, the name was important enough to Flora to be used again when, in 1925, she founded a postal literary club and called it the Peverel Society.

The new Flora Thompson of Peverel was much less precious than the old, and more confident in her style and in the statement of her opinions. Fiona still makes an occasional appearance, but Boojie and Father Conlan do not. Such references as she makes to her childhood imply that she came of a reasonably well-to-do family; when she describes the harvest-home feast (see page 151 below) she explains her knowledge of it by saying that "once, as a child staying at a farm in the Midlands, I had the good fortune to be in the fun of one". But many of the affections in the "Out of Doors" articles are allowed to disappear. In due course more and more references to the world of Lark Rise begin to occur, and the actual names of Lark Rise characters – "Old Sally", "Queenie" – are seen for the first time.† And Flora shows increasing confidence in her knowledge and experience of the natural history and wild life of the area.

---

* It is unlikely that she was trying to put local people off the scent. Already in May 1921 the publisher of her book of poems, *Bog-Myrtle and Peat,* had placed an advertisement for the book next to her "Out of Doors" article, describing her as "post-mistress in a small Hampshire village". Local readers of the *Catholic Fireside* could hardly have been deceived.

†Her brother Edwin Timms had already been rechristened Edmund in "Out of Doors in July".

Her model in this respect was Gilbert White. Selborne is only a mile or two beyond Woolmer Forest, and her frequent references to his work show that she had read him thoroughly. In many respects her methods – patient and detailed observation combined with a sceptical, enquiring mind – were similar to his. In addition she had read Linnaeus, Huxley and Darwin, as well as more or less contemporary and local nature-writers like W. H. Hudson and the poet Coventry Patmore.

It is tempting to try and identify the "mere snail-shell" of a cottage below Peverel Down in which these 72 articles are set, particularly since at one stage (February to June 1921) they are actually accompanied by photographs which must have been taken by Flora or by a friend on her behalf. One of these photographs is captioned "a corner of the cottage", another "the valley stream". But one must reckon with Flora's powers to deceive, for although the cottage in the photograph is indeed identifiable,* it does not correspond in every other respect with her descriptions – which are themselves mutually contradictory! The truth is that she attached her yearning for solitude and rural bliss to a number of places both around Liphook and in the New Forest. These imagined idylls are mixed together with her much more rigorous descriptions of the natural scenery and wild life of the Liphook area. Her recorded conversations with shepherds, gipsies and others are probably often invented, for they are reminiscent of similar dialogue purporting to have been recalled after half a century in *Lark Rise to Candleford*; but they always shed light on some real issue, such as the plight of the rural poor, or worrying changes in local conditions for wild life, or whatever might be the author's concern at the time. The final proof of the accuracy of Flora Thompson's observations of the locality is simply that, as at Juniper Hill and Cottisford in Oxfordshire, the local people of Liphook can, today, recognise their landscape in her descriptions.

The Peverel Society, founded in 1925, seems to have flourished for some years. It began in 1924 as a reading circle in the pages of the *Catholic Fireside*, comprising an essay by Flora on some literary topic and readers' competitions in verse and prose. After a year these columns ended, and the Society replaced them. The following is the full text of an advertisement appearing in the *Catholic Fireside* in March 1926:

---

*The cottage in the photograph is known as Foley Lodge, just off the A3 a mile south of Liphook. Peverel Down is Weaver's Down, which stretches south-west from Griggs Green on the B2131 west of Liphook. Another cottage with which Flora seems to have identified is Spring Pond Cottage, north of Bramshott. Other identifications are given in the footnotes to the text.

Can You Write?

IF SO, DO NOT BURY YOUR
TALENT, but have it trained by means
of one of our Courses.

SHORT STORY WRITING.

Complete Course of Six Lessons, with
revision of Pupil's own efforts and advice
as to placing with Editors.

CONDUCTED BY

FLORA THOMPSON, Author of 'Bog-
Myrtle and Peat,' 'The Peverel Papers,'
&c, AND

MYLDREDE HUMBLE-SMITH,
Honours English Language and Litera-
ture, Oxon., B.Litt., Durham.

Terms for the Full Course £1 10 6
(Instalments arranged if desired).

THOSE WHO DO NOT ASPIRE TO WRITE FOR
THE PRESS SHOULD OBTAIN PARTICULARS OF
OUR GENERAL CULTURE COURSE

POETS ARE INVITED TO JOIN THE
PEVEREL SOCIETY.

All Particulars may be obtained from:
MISS FLORA THOMPSON
Ruskin House, Liphook, Hants.*

Later that year the society was advertising "The Peverel Book of Verse", 56 poems by members of the Peverel Society, selected and arranged by Flora Thompson, for sale at 1s 3d. But by the following year the tone had changed somewhat for the worse, and begun to sound a bit like a lonely-hearts club: "There is no need to be lonely! The Peverel Society offers sympathetic criticism to literary aspirants! New friendships and new interests to all!" It is easy to make fun of the Society, but Flora believed strongly in its aims and continued for many years after her departure from Liphook to devote her energies to it.

But before she left, one of her dreams did for a time come true. The Thompsons succeeded in buying a small house on the Longmoor Road out of Liphook, just beyond Griggs Green, at the foot of Weaver's Down and on the border of Woolmer Forest. This was the very heart of Peverel.† Yet inexplicably – or perhaps understandably since he was never himself a true

---

*One cannot help noticing minor falsehoods in this copy: Flora was no "Miss"; her house next to the post office was not and never had been called "Ruskin House"; and it has proved impossible to trace a Humble-Smith among holders of the B.Litt degree from Durham University.

†The house is still there, much as it looked in Flora's day. But it has been joined by numerous modern neighbours.

country-man – John Thompson promptly put in for promotion in the postal service and was almost immediately transferred to Dartmouth. Flora, however, was able to postpone her departure for over a year, on the pretext of selling the house; and for this period she must have been able to live a life quite like the one she had for so many years imagined and idealised. It could all be found in a poem she had written long ago in her Bournemouth days, and included in *Bog-Myrtle and Peat*. It is entitled "Earthly Paradise", and includes the line:

"When I am old,
    Give me for heaven a little house set on a heath . . ."

Flora Thompson's life can be seen, and may have been seen by her, as a succession of missed opportunities and unfulfilled yearnings. Already in her early teens she was showing an affinity for culture and education which no one in her community shared. She had from the start a strong sense of independence of view, and in her own words found it constantly "mortifying to be reminded that one has neither the birth, education, nor any personal quality to justify the holding of an opinion differing from those held by the majority". All her life she felt some fine destiny was awaiting but always somehow just eluding her. The gipsy she met and described in "Out of Doors in November" (1921) "was certainly able to read the secret desire, for she promised me love and praise and friendship!"*

In Grayshott, when she was still in her early twenties and had not even met John Thompson, she had imagined the plot of a novel to be called "Dodder". Far out on the moors there was a patch of heather which looked stunted; "when closely examined every individual plant could be seen to be netted and dragged down to earth by the thin, red, threadlike runners of a parasite plant" called dodder. The novel would be "the story of a woman of fine, sensitive nature, bound by marriage to one of a nature which was strong, coarse, and encroaching, and would tell how, in time, the heather person shrank and withered, while the dodder one fattened and prospered"†

There was also the unfulfilled affair with "Richard Brownlow", described

---

*See *A Country Calendar and other writings* edited by Margaret Lane (Oxford University Press, 1979), page 131. This book contains as its Introduction Miss Lane's biographical essay on Flora Thompson, to which I am indebted for some of the facts about her life given here. It also includes the text of *Heatherley*.

†Dodder is described in the text below, page 159. The plot of the novel is discussed with Richard and Mavis Brownlow in *Heatherley*, chapter VIII.

with great feeling in *Heatherley*. But most poignant of all, perhaps, is this invented personality, a Flora whose father was a doctor and whose aunts made samplers, a Flora of birth and breeding who could afford to decide by herself to give up the world of "getting and spending" and become the "Hermit of Peverel Downs".

In the long run, many of Flora's literary ambitions were fulfilled. She lived to see the publication of her trilogy, and to see it greatly praised by leading literary figures. But success came too late and she seems to have had little enjoyment from its fruits. Living in retirement in a cottage at Brixham, she was too old to be taken up by the *literati,* to welcome a visit from Father Conlan or an introduction to the Poet.

Yet her work has truly lasting value. In *Lark Rise to Candleford* we recognise a uniquely authentic portrait of rural life at the end of its golden age, and "of that more excellent way of life of our forefathers". In *The Peverel Papers* these great qualities are already discernible; many of the recollections of which *Lark Rise* is composed are already here, sometimes in more detail. In addition there is a great deal of marvellously observant natural history writing.

What makes Flora Thompson such a good writer is the combination of passion and control. We are never unaware of the fire that burns beneath the robust common sense of her outlook. In her account of discovering wild lilies of the valley in a remote Oxfordshire wood in her youth, witnessed only by a singing blackbird (page 124), we feel the power of her love for that landscape and the ache of her nostalgia. Her recollections of the rare sighting of the kingfisher are so beautifully written that we cannot fail to share what these experiences meant to her. Her fascinating and intricate descriptions of flower mechanisms (the bluebell, the broom), or of the methods of nest-building employed by different species of bird, or of the architecture of the red anthill, make us aware of the many hours of close and devoted observation that were needed to reach such understanding, and of the price she paid. Unlike Gilbert White, she was no well-to-do country vicar, with only a few souls in his care and a sermon to write for Sunday; and her skills had been acquired at great cost.

The question lying at the core of her work, and never conclusively answered, is whether the way of life of our forefathers was truly more excellent than our own. Over and over again the comparison is made. In the past, country people had "an easy conscience, unshaken faith, a margin of spiritual energy". People today no longer had the capacity to be happy with little. And yet she never comes near to rejecting the present or the advantages of progress. She knows that religious faith was already less secure even in her own youth, and that country labourers were shamelessly exploited. She knew this even when she was herself still a child, as the touching account of her embarrassment during the harvest-home feast (see pages 152-3) makes clear. She is the first to appreciate the advantages of local bus services, and the advances in medical care. And yet, inescapably, she teaches us what we have lost in winning these gains.

In all Flora Thompson's work, and particularly here, a most lovable, sensible and sensitive personality is revealed. We shall learn little more about her than she was able to reveal in her published writings, for no new contemporary witnesses are likely to come to light. But these qualities are abundantly displayed in *The Peverel Papers,* and will continue to attract readers to her books.

*   *   *

The 72 Peverel Papers, published monthly over six years, amount in all to some quarter of a million words. To fit them for publication in book form some selection has been necessary. I have attempted to represent the full width of Flora Thompson's interests, to avoid repetition, and to satisfy interest in the links between this work and her better-known books. In addition, since some passages from these papers have already been republished, under the title *A Country Calendar,* I have usually excluded material that is already available in print. I have also attempted, as explained above, to identify in footnotes some of the places that Flora lightly disguised, so that visitors and local people in the Liphook area may retrace her steps on Peverel Downs.

In Liphook there is no lack of appreciation of the Flora Thompson connection, and I am grateful to Laurence Giles of the Bramshott and Liphook Preservation Society for his help in my researches in the area. His Society has erected a fine bronze bust of Flora Thompson in front of the new post office, and a commemorative plaque on the house next door to the old one – the house where the Thompsons lived for eleven years, and where Flora wrote these papers.

January

January

SOME GREAT POET or philosopher once said that "he who goes to nature for comfort must go to her empty-handed", and I think he was right.

Not that I myself had ever much to relinquish, and that which I had, excepting a bare subsistence, the war took from me; but even the very little which is left to me seems at times to come between myself and perfect tranquility. No doubt it is just as well that it should be so; it was ordained that our earthly pilgrimage should be a struggle, and life would be a tame affair if everything went smoothly.

Yet, on the whole, life does go more smoothly with me than it does with most people. It was not always so. For some time after the armistice had put an end to my war service I remained in the press of things, getting and spending. Then, suddenly, the futility of it all was revealed to me, and, clutching faith and courage as one who had great need of them, I dared to simplify my own life by cutting down my needs to a minimum.

By what we humans call accident, I came upon this cottage, a mere snail-shell of a place, so small and low and grey, tucked away amongst pine and holly at the foot of the Peverel Downs.

By the shores of a little lake, a few yards farther up the valley, tradition says, a holy hermit once had his dwelling. A narrow lane leading down to the shore still bears his name; the lake itself is called "Hermit's Pool". But all memory of what manner of man he was, whence he came, or in what particular way his sanctity was made manifest, has perished. Being interested in such legends, I came one summer day to gather together and record such fragmentary traces as remained; but as soon as I saw that peaceful hollow in the downs, the wood, the leaf-reflecting pool, the little grey cottage with the blue hills behind, the billowing heath before, my mission was forgotten. I felt like a homing bird after a stormy flight, and could only lie in the grass and fern resting war-worn nerves and steeping my tired soul in the beauty and peace of it all.

I spent one day in thinking and planning, another in searching out and making terms with the owner of the place, and many more in putting it in order, for it had been long unoccupied and neglected; but, at last, all was done,

and I settled here, a modern hermit, with my dog and my books for company, my garden to supply my frugal table, and my pen to provide my simple luxuries.

The struggle had been breathless. At first my spirit was faint and languid; my body, dismayed at the hardships and inconveniences of such primitive conditions, easily cast down and sorrowful. But, gradually, there stole upon me all the comfort and healing nature holds in store for such stripped ones; my little cell became dear to me, my garden provided both discipline and pleasure, the keen moorland air revivified my body, the silence and solitude my soul and brain.

Not that I had not still my moments of weakness. Sometimes, at first, on dark winter nights, when the wind rushed over the downs and shrilled through the pine-trees, and all manner of strange noises were abroad, I would imagine the sound of footsteps in the driven leaves, and shrink with the sudden unreasoning dread of a woman living, for the first time in her life, alone.

Since then I have spent two years here. I have steeped my whole being in the rain and dew, have rejoiced in the sun, exulted in the shrilling of the wind. The song of birds, the stirring of insects, the murmuring of bees in the heath-bells, of wandering winds in the tree-tops, the crackling of snow and frost, the plashing of summer rain – every one of nature's myriad voices has struck an answering chord in me. I have come to love the loose, warm, peaty soil of this southern county, and wish for no better fate than to live and die here.

But it is not good that man, still less woman, should live to themselves alone. The work of healing completed, my heart turns to my own kind again. I have neighbours, of course, dwellers in the cottages dotted about the heath; simple, kindly folk, always ready to stop work for a cheery word with the passer-by. I have come to know some of the village people, too; the gift of sympathy, the one gift with which God has endowed me, which in other days, in the outside world, brought me many strange confidences, has not lain wholly dormant. But they have their interests, I have mine; our intercourse, excepting in rare moments of stress, does not go much farther than an exchange of weather prophecy.

But, farther afield, scattered world-wide, are others, men and women who love the things I love – the small, beautiful, simple things in nature and in life. For these I will write and send out these papers, telling them of all I see and hear and read which I think will interest them, hoping that, before very long, they will come to think of the Hermit of Peverel Downs as a friend . . .

This morning the long wavy ridge of the Downs at the back of my house was snow-capped. Usually they are but faintly blue, showing green turf and dark encircling hedgerows only before heavy rain, turning to piled-up amethyst at sunset, obliterated altogether in fog and mist. But to-day the crisp, clear atmosphere reflecting the snow drew them quite near, so near that I felt tempted to walk straight off to them, although I knew, in sober geographical fact, six miles of bog and heath and field and village lay between.

The smaller, nearer hill, which keeps guard over Peverel Heath, wore its winter white with a difference. With its heath and furze ruffling the snow-drifts, it was shaggy, black and white, and looked more like a crouching, watchful animal than ever. This hill is heather-clad; the farther ones are chalk and turf and wild-thyme. From them, people say, you can see the sea; we cannot, because they close us in, but often I fancy I can scent it.

That is on mild, wet, windy days. Not on such mornings as this, when, even in the long narrow wood which shelters with me beneath the hill, there was scarce a stir, unless when one of the pines freed itself from its snowy burden, and the slow, sliding fall of it re-echoed long through the sharp, clear silence.

That and the "Yaff! Yaff!" of a woodpecker were the only sounds. The smaller birds kept very quiet in such weather; they need all their energy, poor birdies, just to keep a spark of life in their tiny, cold-puffed bodies. They came very humped and shivering to their breakfast of soaked bread – two chaffin-ches, ten sparrows, a missle-thrush, a robin, and Gulliver amongst the

Lilliputians, a carrion crow, one of a pair which haunt my steps each time I climb the hill, settling upon a bush or tree-stump a few yards in advance and flapping away with melancholy croakings each time I draw near.

Yesterday I had an even wilder guest, for a hare came at noonday and invited himself to dine upon my winter spinach. I had not the heart to "Shoo!" him away – although I, too, like spinach, and his appetite was truly alarming – for he looked so pretty, sitting up upon his haunches and eating daintily, like a well-behaved child at table, scanning the windows all the time with dark, innocent, cold-glazed eyes.

He was a stranger-guest, but the birds are always with me, for the wood, although narrow, is a tentacle of a much larger one running out of Hampshire into Sussex and locating itself at last in the dim blue mistiness of the weald. Not only that, but the Hermit's Pool and my garden with the oak and chestnut trees closing them round form an oasis in the dry, sandy darkness of the heath. Birds on the wing sight it from far above, and drop down for rest and refreshment. In this way I have become acquainted, at one time and another, with almost every bird known in this country, from the swan and wild-goose upon the pool to the wren and tree-climber which haunt the underwood.

As I brushed the snow from my porch and doorway and stopped to beat my numbed hands together for warmth, the heath beyond my little white gate lay freezing in utter silence. Not a creature was in sight. Yes, one; one whose presence explained the absence of all others. Against the greyish-dun of the sky, suspended like a biplane, hung a kestrel. Moment after moment he remained quite stationary, until some current of the upper air upset his balance and he sailed with staccato wing-beatings down the wind and the little birds were free to come out from their hiding-places.

Across the dark heath the path wound ankle-deep; illuminated by the winter-whiteness, the eye could trace it a mile or more to where it drops beneath the railway arch and becomes one with the road which leads to Rome, to London, or merely and more often to Peverel village.*

*This is still an accurate description of the Sussex Border path where it crosses the railway line at Ripsley.

I cross this path almost daily, sometimes cycling, but more often on foot, for sandy ways make heavy going for wheels, to make my frugal purchases at the village shop, to collect my letters and newspaper, or to change my library book at the station bookstall . . .

To-day has been one of those rare blue and white and golden days which sometimes come at this time of year sandwiched between a score of dun and steely-grey ones.

At daybreak the sun, a flat red disc, reflected itself upon the thin white ice of the Hermit's Pool. The clustering trees, dark and icy still, stood sharply against a copper sky. Underfoot the herbage was crisp and springy to the tread, every separate blade and leaf encrusted and edged with filigree frost-work. A great hush was upon everything. The trees, lately so strained and tossed with tempest, were still; even the pines, never wholly silent, had subsided to a murmur.

Against the sharp, clear stillness, sounds at ordinary times too subtle for human hearing became plainly audible; the footfall of the thrush, searching the frozen earth for food; the whispering of the sere leaves upon the oak; the fairy tinkling of the rime as it slid from branch to branch of the pine; all seemed part of a delicate undertone only to be caught for an instant in the hush caused by the suspension of coarser sounds.

Down by the Pool rang a tiny tapping as though some belated fairy frostworker still tarried at his anvil. "Tink! Tink! Tonk!" Then a sharp crack and a gurgle of water; the moorhen had broken through the thin ice with her bill.

She was not permitted to enjoy her draught in peace. Scarcely had she taken

a sip, rolled her eyes and elevated her beak with the queer, ecstatic gulping motion birds have when drinking, before the wild ducks came trundling in single file from the reed-bed. How they tumbled over each other, and broke the ice with their weight, and wallowed and muddied the water, until the moorhen's fairy drinking-fountain was a muddy trough for yards beneath the bank! Finally, the moorhen, sharing the fate of pioneers in general, was driven from the spot with pecks and hisses, while the valley, with all that splashing and squawking going on, became anything but silent!

Later in the day, as the sun gathered strength, most of the fairy frostwork melted into thin air. Not quite all of it; there was too keen an edge on the sunshine, but, while one side of a tree or hedge enjoyed an atmosphere like that of early spring, the other side cast a frozen shadow, mimicking its outline upon the grass in frost-crystals. All day the air had a wonderful lightness and buoyancy; it was like drinking a sharp, clear, tasteless wine to inhale it. Walking was pure pleasure; ten, fifteen, even twenty miles did not seem impossible in that atmosphere.

I started off quite early in the day, intending to climb to that last outpost of my walks abroad from which a glimpse of the sea, a faint silvery streak, may be caught between the distant purple of the hills. As so often happens when one has proposed so much, I accomplished very little. At this time of year, when the outdoor hours are so limited, and yet there is so much of interest to see, it is difficult to travel far from one's own door; and I had got no farther than the little farm tucked away at the foot of Peverel when the first unmistakable voice of spring took me out of my way to investigate.

In a sheltered corner, between high hedges, a sheep-fold had been made for the lambing mothers; a cosy thatched and padded den filled to the brim with soft, sweet-smelling hay. Above the deep baa-ing chorus of the elders floated the thin wailing cry of the newly-born.

I stopped to congratulate the old shepherd upon such early arrivals, and he brought the first of the flock, one upon each arm, for me to see. Touchingly weak and helpless they looked with their long, limp, dangling legs and questing nozzles. The mother-sheep, from her bed beneath the penthouse, kept watch upon my every movement, giving a long admonitory "Ba-a-a!" when I put out my hand to caress the damp, soft fleece of the smallest; nor did she seem at all happy until they had snuggled down into the hay by her side again.

The shepherd was extremely proud to display such fine twins before the first month of the year was out; in another week or two the tender bleat of them will come upon the damp air from every farm, but at present each arrival is an event, a subject for talk and wonderment. The old man was much amused at my fearing the cold for them:

"Bless you!" he chuckled, "them's warm enough! Look at this pen, now; furze to keep cold out, and hay to keep warmth in. That's my motto in lambin' time, same's 'twas my father's afore me. No. Wind and cold you *can* fight; 'tis rain and fog as be the enemies. You knows where you are in such weather as this is; but in damp, muggy weather you *don't* know!"

I left him at the turnip mill, grinding out a sweet-smelling creamy pulp for his charges' dinner, as happy and busy a man as could be found upon earth. Yet he had been up half the night attending to the twins and their mother, and had the prospect of many more such nights before him in the immediate future. It is difficult to picture a town workman putting in so many hours for so little pay as he does. The secret, I suppose, is a genuine vocation; he loves the work, and loves the living creatures under his care, and all the rest is easy . . .

The ivy, even more than the holly, is Winter's own plant; for not only does it fruit, but it flowers also, between Michaelmas and Easter. Last of all native plants to flower, and first in the year to fruit, it provides a feast in a meagre time, first for the moths and bees, then for the birds. Right over Christmas, as long as the mealy pollen dust upon the flowers lasts, you will find upon any mild day a host of winged things of all sizes hovering and sipping at it, hurrying and buzzing and tumbling all the time as though they realised how short the day was and how certain the frost at the end of it.

The enemies of the ivy, woodmen, suburban gardeners and the like, greatly exaggerate its harmful influence upon whatever tree may happen to support it. The ivy, according to them, is a kind of vampire of the woods, taking the noble oak or elm into a deadly stranglehold and gradually crushing the life from it.

There is a tincture of truth in this belief. Upon light-limbed, scanty-foliaged trees, such as the birch or the mountain-ash, the growth of the ivy is always harmful, for it is a plant which loves light, and upon trees which do not give sufficient shade to keep it in check it will flourish only too well, and end by overtopping and destroying its unfortunate host. But upon the forest giant, oak or elm, or, more rarely, the beech, it will do no harm, but stand entwined like wedded king and queen, a joy to all beholders for centuries.

The only other vivid green in the woods this month is furnished by the mosses. This month and next is the flowering time of many of the species, and upon stump and stone and twined amongst the stems of bush and briar are fairy forests of emerald plumes, some with hairy dark-red flower-cups, quite discernible by the unassisted eye; others dusted with yellow bloom, a butter-cup meadow to each square inch, if our human sight were but subtle enough to discern it.

As I stepped very softly and silently over a carpet of it in the depth of the pinewood, I came face to face with a perching mass of yellowy-white feathers, almost on a level with my eyes. It was a barn-owl, and was, I think, asleep when I first came upon it; but even when it opened first one, then the other, of its

round wide eyes, it seemed to look through rather than at me, and did not offer to stir.

It looked so quaint, sitting and blinking there close to the tree-trunk, opening and shutting its eyes alternately, swaying and recovering its balance the while, like an elderly lady taking a surreptitious doze in the midst of the family circle, that at first I was amused; but when I saw how wet and draggled its plumage was, and how weakly it swayed backwards and forwards upon its low perch, I knew that misery and exhaustion had made it so tame, and was sorry for it.

The poor bird was probably homeless for the workmen had been busy close by all the week and had brought down, amongst other trees, an immense hollow oak trunk, which had been the headquarters of its kindred from time immemorial.

I turned aside to look at it. Very melancholy in its fall and decay, it lay across the mossy path, a mere shell of a thing. After its life of a thousand years or more, it must have stood stark and rotting in the earth for centuries, for all round the platform of its pollarded head were little terraced gardens, bird planted, springing with ferns and mosses and honeysuckle and briar festoons, the latter so long established they fell almost to the earth, and draped the naked trunk like a head of hair. The secret chambers where the owls had nested were open to the day; wads of hay and wool and feathers were strewn upon the earth around. Amongst them were more ghastly relics, masses of small bones, pellets of fur, and the almost intact skeleton of some small animal.

Why the particular owl I saw skulking near had not found for itself a new shelter is rather a puzzle. Probably it had been injured in some way, perhaps by a carelessly flung stone, for, sleeping as it would by day, it will almost certainly be at home when the house-breakers arrived. Of its companions in misfortune there was no trace; but, as I took my last look at heath and sky to-night, there seemed to be a strangely human note of trouble and bereavement in the long "Too-woo-whoot!" which sounded so lingeringly upon the frosty air . . .

Beneath the garden fruit trees three golden eyes looked up through leafless boughs at the sun. My one treasured clump of winter aconite had revived at the first breath of warmth. All the time the frost had held sway the golden petals had drooped limply over the delicately-notched waxen green of the leaves; now the three small cups were held up to catch the sunbeams like morsels of midsummer fallen into the lap of January.

It is a wonder this one flower of mid-winter is so seldom seen in our gardens, coming as it does before even the snowdrop dares. At Kew, I am told, they have a large patch of it under some trees, but I have never happened to be there at the time they were in bloom, and until I came here to live scarcely knew it by sight.

Perhaps the reason that it is so little cultivated is that it is of wilful growth, thriving only where it chooses, with no settled regard for soil or aspect. Often, in old gardens, a stray tuft or two may be seen under a fruit tree or by a wall in a grassy margin, and there it will remain for a lifetime, never increasing, yet never wholly disappearing, while deliberately planted roots a few yards away are never seen a second season.

Upon Peverel, it has a footing in most of the older cottage gardens, springing up year after year directly after Christmas, blooming and dying down, dug over and forgotten for the rest of the year. This unanimity may not be altogether coincidence, for the winter aconite has a history behind it. To our Saxon ancestors it was known as the wolf's-bane; and in a district so wolf-infested as to be named after them as this forest of Woolmer was the wolf's-bane may have been cultivated either as a balm for wounds or a charm to scare the creatures themselves away.

In the garden during the last few months a slow, silent invasion has been going on. First of all, a pale green splash appeared upon some edging stones which had been brought from a distance. This proved upon examination to be flat mossy growth, which soon ran the whole length of the border, climbed the stone trough of the pump, and fledged it delicately, finally spreading itself over a rockery under the window and extending to the flagstones of the path.

At first I mistook it for a lichen, although no lichen was ever so translucently emerald; but, after tracking it through book after book, I found it was one of those heptacaeas of which the old herbalist Gerard wrote: "They do grow in moist and shady places where the sunbeams seldom penetrate and no traveller frequenteth." He goes on to say that "it is a singularly good remedy against inflammations of the liver", a belief which together with the shape of the scales which do duty for leaves, no doubt earned for it its popular name of liver-wort.

He wrote in the age of faith, when

"Everything green which came out of the mould
Was an excellent herb to our fathers of old,"

and from the shape and colour of a plant they were able to read, by the doctrine of signatures, as they styled it, its appointed use in the art of healing. In this way red flowers and berries were concluded to be good for the blood; wide-open bright blue flowers were a sovereign balm for eye trouble; heart-shaped leaves were supposed to cure a weak heart; liver-shaped ones, such as these, were a remedy for liver disorder.

The liver-wort has no place in the modern pharmacopoeia; its ony mission now is to delight the eye and refresh the soul of man. This it does to perfection for no fern in a tropical forest could be more delicately fashioned or more pellucidly green than these tiny fronds, so infinitesimally small, yet massed in such perfect loveliness . . .

This morning's sunrise was one to remember for years. Above the red disc in the east, a curtain of crimson and flame-coloured clouds hung from the zenith; the rest of the sky was rose-tinted with reflected light, and a strange, unearthly glow was upon all things.

The postman, passing on his round, called out that the sky was "a nasty colour"; and, in answer to my protesting smile, patted the rolled-up water-proof slung from his shoulder.

"I shall want this before I get half-way round," he explained.

The man must be a magician. Almost before he was out of sight, a low, hissing wind swept through the dried heath-bells; the colour of the cloud-curtain faded to dun, and almost immediately it was raining. As the daylight increased, the wind gathered force, and leisured people rising to a nine o'clock breakfast found a wild and stormy world beyond their windows.

All day upon the heath the dead bracken-fronds have been ruffled into waves; the pine trees upon the summit have been bowed in the wind, or tossed like waving feathers in the rainstorms. Against the driving masses of cloud scarce a wing has appeared; if a bird has attempted to rise, it has been so set upon and buffeted by the wind that, after battling a moment or two, it has dropped like a stone. Even the rooks have been tossed like black balls before the storm.

To-night, after the steely glint of a watery sunset, the gale has freshened; the wind is roaring through the wood and howling round the cottage, shaking the doors and pelting the windows and sending the raindrops sizzling down the chimney into the fire.

Heard from within, the tumult of the woods is like the rushing of waters, a hundred storm-voices blended into one hoarse roar. Heard out of doors and close at hand, the sounds are distinguishable, there is the voice of the wind itself, rushing and raving across the earth like a giant let loose; the roaring of the tree-tops as it bows or releases them; the crashing and straining of branches, and the snapping of twigs.

Between the gusts come sobbing and sighing sounds – the drifting of dead leaves, the gurgling of water, or the pattering of raindrops upon the ever-greens. For the acute listener there are other and more mysterious noises – dull reverberations of earth, like the sound of human footsteps; shrill, child-like screams of strained branches moving back into place; sudden, abrupt sighs of stray winds in the undergrowth.

Startling as some of these sounds may be to the nervous, there is nothing to fear. Every single sound may be traced to either wind or water. The birds are huddled in the depths of the thickest underwood, the smaller four-footed things sleep on in their grass-lined crannies, unaware of the storm. Even the fox goes hungry rather than face the weather, no living creature moves abroad in these solitudes on such a night, least of all, man...

Across the clearing, jays flash with loud wing-beats and harsh, defiant-sounding screams, the blue of their wing-feathers gleaming like steel against the darkness of the pines. Although not reckoned amongst flocking-birds they are seldom seen singly, but fly in companies of two to five – probably family parties, for it is supposed they keep together, parents and children, until with the spring the young ones separate to found families of their own.

The jay is an exception to the general rule of "no storehouse nor barn" among birds, for it has a habit of hiding quite considerable collections of acorns for its winter use. These, with worms and grubs and the last pickings of wild berries, keep it impudent and flourishing while other birds starve.

Sometimes, in the older parts of the woods where the trees are hoary with decay, the woodpecker may be heard sounding the bark of the trunks for hollow spots where insects may be found. The sound of its hammering comes muffled and dull compared to the clear "Tap! Tap!" which rings through the woods from its bill in summer; for the decayed wood soaks up rain like a sponge and sounds heavy and sodden. Now and again, but very rarely, the green woodpecker may be glimpsed, green with a glint of crimson about the head, as it zig-zags about a lichened trunk, tapping continuously until a hollow spot is struck, when it sets to work to strip off the bark and devour the meal which its skill has laid bare.

Occasionally it descends to earth and rifles one of the large, loosely-piled hills of the wood-ants for a change of diet, darting its long, strong bill in and out the soft mass of earth and twigs in a way that speaks plainly of wholesale slaughter. It would be strange indeed if the woodpecker wanted for food, for it is better equipped for obtaining it than almost any other bird; not only is its bill a strong tool for hammering, probing, and stripping bark, but it is supplemented by a still longer tongue – a slender, supple instrument, furnished with rows of small barbs like the teeth of a rake. By means of this combination of implements the woodpecker can reach and extract insects and larvae which lurk in the most seemingly inaccessible nooks . . .

This time of general overhead leaflessness is the best of all the year for observing the tree-shapes. Standing out against a misty grey or a snowy landscape, our woodland and hedgerow trees take on a different character, as distinct from that of their leafiness as the etching from the oil painting. Colour has given place to form; trunks stand out in firm and majestic outline; twigs and branches are interlaced in a clear, sharp tracery; swelling buds show dark and rounded against the sky. Not that colour is altogether lacking; each tree is etched in its own distinctive tint – greyish-brown for the oak, purple for the birch and the beech; and so on through a hundred gradations of the different shades.

There is no need at this time of year to examine a tree closely in order to identify it. The far-off forms can be distinguished at a glance – the oak, short and massive of trunk and branching at the fork to a spreading head of many boughs; the elm, with a certain resemblance to the oak, but more graceful, dividing at the fork into two or three main limbs, then soaring rather than spreading. Then the ash, with its smoother outline and few, sparsely-set boughs; the beech, like a cathedral pillar; the poplar, pointing skyward, and so on, to that delicate lady of the woods, the silver birch, with its gleaming white stem and tracery of purple twigs.

Nor, even at this barest of seasons, is the earth utterly flowerless. At every breath of mild air, dandelions and daisies peer up from the turf; violets and primroses open singly in sheltered garden nooks; the lesser celandine in the lanes opens a golden eye to the sun, or turns the papery white of closed petals to the wind. All of them smile upon winter's face, the more precious for their rarity . . .

To-day has been such a day of promise, from the moment a broad red streak of dawn made a frieze of the birch twigs with the tiny, dark, puffed-up balls of sleeping birds as fruit, and the marsh mist lay flat, like a white sheet upon the heath, through alternate hours of showers and mild sunshine to the dusk with its earth-scents and misty stars.

"Muggy weather! Not what I should call wholesome," declared the very neighbour who complained so bitterly of the keen, frosty wind a day or two back – a wind which, according to him, came direct from the North Pole and pierced the thick furze and straw of his lambing-fold like shots from a gun.

That kind of weather was bad for his newly-born lambs, and this bad for his own kind. "A green Christmas, a fat churchyard," he reminded me gloomily, and it would only have provoked further complaints to have reminded him that Christmas is far behind us and the earth spinning on towards the longest day.

The man is a confirmed weather-critic. I firmly believe he had his expensive wireless set installed for the sole purpose of checking the weather forecasts and finding them incorrect. For him, it is always too sharp or too mild, too windy or too stagnant; in all the years I have lived near him I have never known him satisfied. If showers in May promise a bumper hay crop, he still grieves lest it should be gathered in too damp and the rick fire!

As a matter of fact, the weather of to-day suited him perfectly, and he was out for two hours before breakfast arranging his men's work so that the mild spell should be taken advantage of; just as last week, while he grumbled about the frosty wind, he took good care to cart manure on to his fields while the ground was frozen too hard for the wheels to sink in the mud of the lanes.

But, after all, he is but a caricature of us all in our weather-criticising moods. "This abominable English climate!" his landlord declares when the scent is poor upon a hunting morning. "Lovely weather for wash-day, I *don't* think!" his carter's wife calls to her neighbour over the fence as she pegs her clothes on the line.

The question is, what do we require of this much-abused climate of ours in Winter? Some people bewail the "good old times" when the coaches were snowed up and they roasted whole oxen upon the ice of the Thames; others shrink from even moderate cold and envy those who can afford to fly to Egypt or the South of France. Few, indeed, are ready to take the weather as it comes, enjoy the good times, make the best of the bad times, and thank God for the beauty of earth and sky.

It is, indeed, these very atmospheric changes which keep our islands so fresh and green and strew our woods and fields with the wildflowers we are so justly proud of. While prolonged frost and snow leave the earth-colours blanched and sodden, such short spells as we are subject to only seem to brighten and freshen.

Even in this second week in January, the rich brown of the furrowed fields is chequered with blue-green squares of winter-sown wheat. The heath is full of colour – tawny gold of the wet sand-spits, the copper and rusts of the dead bracken fronds, the rough red of pine stems, and the pinkish silver of birch.

In the woods, the mosses and lichens brighten the boles of the forest trees and form soft cushions and carpets of bright colour at their feet. This is the flowering season of many of our native species, and many an old wall, ditch-side, or woodland bank is a garden in miniature. The non-flowering mosses, too, revived by the moisture, are fuller and brighter than at any other time of year. Such glinting of smooth velvet tufts on outhouse roofs! Such feathery forests of fairy fronds beneath the bushes!

Even the sphagnum of the marshes, left high and dry and blanched to the semblance of carved ivory in the Autumn, has now had time to soak itself back to its own delicate green. If there were nothing more worth going out to see just now, the mosses alone would make a Winter walk worth while....

One species which may be seen everywhere, even in the heart of towns, is that sensitive plant among mosses, the Screw Moss, which may now be seen blooming upon almost any wall-top in town or country. If the flowers are examined closely, some of them will be found wearing little hoods of a brownish colour, while others have shed this protective covering and show

the little red teeth which give the rust-red tinge to the brown. If the weather is sunny, these red teeth will be seen standing erect from the mouth of the vessel which contains the ripened spores, but in cloudy or damp weather the whole flower twists itself up into a kind of whorl to protect them.

So sensitive is this infinitesimal floret to atmospheric changes that, if breathed upon by the human breath, it will instantly twist up into the tiny screw from which the plant takes its name.

But the Screw Moss is but one of our five hundred native species. The mosses are everywhere – upon the flags of paved city courts; upon walls, roof-tiles and vacant building plots in the suburbs; entwined with the grasses in country meadows; carpeting the woods, and clothing rocks and stones and tree-boles with their living green.

So much has been said and written in praise of the turf which does so much towards making our country the "green and pleasant land" it is, that the share of the mosses in that direction has generally been overlooked. Yet it is told us upon good authority that one-fourth of the total area of our wild open spaces is covered with moss.

We pass these humble plants unnoticed in the general greenery, but in some less fortunate countries they provide the only softening touch of green. In

Tierra del Fuego, the wildest and most desolate spot in the world, perhaps, there are mosses to fleck the naked rock of the otherwise barren wilderness.

Over the Siberian tundras, vast, treeless plains, where, even in Summer, the earth never thaws to more than a few inches from the surface, and grass and wild flowers are unknown, the mosses provide the only form of vegetation. Beneath the dense growth of the tropics; up to the snow line of mountains; in marshes and upon sun-baked deserts the mosses may be found.

Although our British mosses seem at present to serve no other purpose than those of delighting the human eye and furnishing hiding places and habitations for innumerable insects, they have played a most important part in the great scheme of Creation. Long before the higher forms of vegetation could find foothold on the naked rock of the newly-cooled earth's surface the mosses came and throve through countless generations, each small tuft drawing its sustenance from the air, attracting and holding together the dusty particles washed down by the rains, dying and leaving behind it the residue of its decay, until soil enough had collected for higher vegetable life to flourish in.

Servi, or labourers, the great botanist Linnaeus called the mosses – a name of honour – for in the first appearance of the first minute specimen -

> *"a spark of green -*
> *A tiny speck, a tiny spore,*
> *That on the vast savannahs of the shore*
> *Was hardly to be seen,"*

was made visible the promise of

> *"The vastitude of vernal green,*
> *The granaries of autumn gold"*

it was to lead up to...

In the garden, the first snowdrop hangs its head, one of the yearly miracles of Nature -

> *"Born of the breath of Winter, and on his brow*
> *Fixed like a pale and solitary star."*

Where there is one solitary bloom to-day, in a fortnight, if the weather keep mild, there will be dozens.

Usually classed as February's flower – as witness the popular names, "Fair Maids of February", "Candlemas Bells", "Flower of the Purification", and so on through all the lovely list, surely the longest and sweetest any flower has to its credit – throughout the West and the extreme South of England the snowdrop comes in with the New Year.

It is remarkable how true to date in its arrival this first flower of the year is. It may vary in different parts of the country, making its appearance at any time between Christmas and the beginning of March, according to climate, but in each district it is punctual to the time it usually appears. Of course, in very severe seasons its coming may be delayed, but not so much as might be supposed, for, when frost and snow have retarded its blooming, it springs at the first thaw as by magic, blade and flower appearing almost simultaneously.

This early and sudden blooming is made possible by the stores laid up in the bulb by the previous year's growth. By the end of September development is so far advanced that, if a bulb be cut through, a rudimentary snowdrop with leaves and a flower-bud may be plainly discerned. But a period of rest is required before further development can take place, and for this reason the snowdrop cannot be persuaded to flower before its time, as the daffodil and hyacinth can.

Those who wish to have the snowdrop indoors in all its natural grace, however, may raise the bulbs the moment the leaves appear, and place them in ordinary garden mould in small pots or vases – any small, artistic receptacle will do, for during the short time the bulbs are indoors no drainage is necessary. Of course the sweet, cold, outdoor plant is best of all seen in its natural surroundings, but the above plan is a great improvement upon the cut flower, and will give much pleasure to the invalid or the aged, who are often unable to get out to see it.

It is a good plan, too, when planting the bulbs out of doors, to place them near the doors and in front of the windows of the house we live in, for they bloom at a time when even the robust are not much in the garden, and only to pass them as we go in and out is to miss much of their precious, fugitive beauty.

Some years ago I was living in a house on the outskirts of Bournemouth, one room of which had a French window opening on to a small lawn with a grassy bank running round it. On this bank I planted dozens of clumps of snowdrops, having them brought specially by gipsies from the New Forest, and adding to them year by year. I left the neighbourhood rather hurriedly at midsummer and the snowdrops were forgotten, but mixed with my regrets for my snow-drops the next winter was a certain pleasure in imagining the new tenants' surprise when they found their grassy bank snowed over with the flowers . . .

Much as we humans enjoy each one of these new signs of the coming of Spring, there are other creatures still more sensitive to the least of them. The birds, above all, are affected by weather-changes, and the way they react to any change for the better is a joy to behold.

Yesterday, mute and half-dead, they crouched under cover while a sleety wind drove across the heath and pierced to the very depth of the woods. This morning, before the rest of the world had realised the change, they were flitting and chirping and preening themselves in the open; while, later in the day, a few of the bolder ones were actually flying in pairs.

First sound of all after daybreak was the song of the garden robin. Perched upon a leafless bough, he filled the air with his silvery little trills and warblings. "Get up! Get up!" he seemed to say. "It is warmer-warmer-warmer!" for all the world as though he knew that upon warmer days gardening operations were resumed and a plentiful worm-supply might be expected.

No wonder he knows the ways of the gardener so well, for he is almost certainly one of a brood hatched out in the garden hedge. Our English robin is essentially a home-keeping bird, and in many cases its whole life is spent in one corner of one parish. A few, of course, have to turn out into the world for economic reasons, but they only do so when they are forced, and then they go no farther than the next garden or next field, the only object of their migration being to find a spot where robins are not too plentiful.

This love of home is probably at the root of the unseemly warfare which goes on between robins, even those of one brood. One garden cannot support more than one or two pairs at most, especially as the robin prefers a meat to a vegetable diet and only falls back upon seeds and suchlike foods when worms, grubs, and insects fail. So parents drive away their offspring to fend for themselves; children of one brood fight among themselves for the privilege of remaining, and all contend with outsiders.

February

February

ONE POURING WET morning last week a very bedraggled young gypsy girl knocked at my door.

She had come from beyond the hills, not keeping to any particular path, but making her way over heath and bog as best she could to save herself a mile or two of the longer highway to the town. She had a basket of clothes-pegs and cheap haberdashery upon her arm, but her object in calling upon me was not so much to offer her wares as to beg for an extra garment to protect her from the downpour.

As she sat sipping her cocoa and toasting her sodden, vilely-clad little feet upon my bright steel fender I could scarcely take my eyes from her. Wet and cold and miserably clad as she was, she seemed to fill my clean, plain little room with a kind of glow.

It was not her beauty altogether, although she was beautiful – not pure gypsy, her dark hair had too much bronze in it, her eyes were too softly brown, theirs are hard, sloe-black and unflinching – yet with the swift wild grace, the innocent boldness of the very young of the Romany. But the nature of the spell she cast did not depend upon physical traits; it went deeper, lying more in the warmth of her appeal, her glad confidence in my sympathy and understanding, the quick illumination of her ready smile, her warmly spoken thanks.

I have never met a human being more highly charged with that strange,

39

subtle quality which, for want of a better definition, we call "charm" than that poor gypsy-girl. I left my work, rather urgent work it happened to be, too, for the sake of the pure pleasure of looking at her and listening to the soft, husky, caressing tones of her wholly gypsy voice.

Alas! more than half of the story she told me was pure fiction, for she told tale after tale, contradicting one with another, and weaving a web of deceit around her family and circumstances which, although tangled, was at least transparent. I had not the heart to expose her; instead, I gave her what she desired, fed and dried her, salving my conscience the while by reminding myself that her hunger and half-bare feet at least were genuine, and as I watched her shrink to a speck upon the heath again, felt that I, and not she was the debtor.

I wonder what is the true nature and origin of the spell she and such as she in all ranks and conditions of life are able to cast over us soberer humans?

What is charm?

It is not a moral quality, for some of the greatest saints have had that one thing in common with some of the most reprobate of sinners. It is not intellectual, for no man by much thinking is able to add a grain of it to his personality. One either has it or has it not; it cannot be acquired, or even greatly cultivated. It is not physical even; for, although it sometimes goes with beauty, just as often it goes with downright ugliness of feature. It seems to be something added to the ordinary human personality, an aura, a glow, the gold-dust upon the butterfly's wing, the bloom upon the peach.

Like charity, it is capable of covering a multitude of sins, or virtues, too, from some eyes. It draws love to its possessor as a magnet draws steel; but, alas, it draws envy, hatred and jealousy just as readily.

The aroma of it floats to us down the centuries. St Francis, I am sure, had it, and the unknown monk of Reading who wrote "Summer is a Coming In". Mary Queen of Scots was a notable example of it. Sir Philip Sidney had it, and Charles Lamb and Stevenson, to name but a few at random.

It is shared by the best and noblest and by some of those whom we consider amongst life's failures; but, whatever its possessor may be, there is one thing he is not, he is never cold of heart or narrow of brain, and at that we will leave it!

My gypsy was the only visitor I had for days; for nearly a week it rained. How it rained! The heath in front of my house was a solid wall of driving wet;

day and night the gale crashed through the trees, rattling the boughs upon the roof-tiles and against the windows. The little threadlike stream which trickles down from the hills and empties itself in the Hermit's Pool was swollen to a torrent; the voice of it became insistent, mingling with my thoughts by day and my dreams by night.

To some people it would have been a melancholy time; but to me the hours were golden, for I am by nature such a truant, lured out of doors by every passing breeze or sunbeam, that I have to depend upon such spells of really bad weather to keep me indoors for long enough together to accomplish anything.

Hour after hour, I worked at my desk, the windows blurred with wet, the room firelit, my one companion stretched upon the rug basking his full length, too lazy to do more than growl feebly each time the rosebush lashed the pane.

Between times I made new chintz covers for the furniture; the orange and blue and green of them looks very bright and fresh against the pale yellow of the distempered walls.

When I came here I was strongly tempted to sell all I had and to give the proceeds, with much more besides, to the antique dealers. The long, low-ceiled cottage rooms, one opening into another, seemed to call aloud for old oak and polished brass. There was just room in the small entry for a monk's bench; a recess in the living-room seemed made on purpose for a grandfather's clock.

From that particular form of house-pride which so artistically apes humility I was delivered by the lightness of my purse. A few tentative enquiries soon showed how very costly such delightful methods of simplifying life can be. So, out of the shabby, comfortable higgledy-piggledy, inherited and acquired, of my household goods I selected the simplest and most useful, and, lo, I had my reward! No sooner were they in their places than they seemed to fit the cottage as a glove fits a hand; they looked as though they had grown there. And now I would not exchange my deep, comfortable chairs and miscellaneous other things for all the rush seats and spindle legs in Liberty's.

This afternoon, just as my oasis between the hills seemed in danger of becoming one vast lake, with myself as a second and very incompetent Noah, quite suddenly it stopped: the clouds rolled aside and piled themselves into a snowy mountain range upon the horizon, the sun came out, and even the poor, drenched birds began to hop and chirp again.

Although it was near sunset and my solitary cup of tea invited me I could not resist the chance of a run in the fresh air. From the heath and downs the fog had lifted, and far-away fields showed green upon the distant hills; out of sight in the clean-washed sky a lark was already soaring and singing. But, under the trees, down by the pool, it was still wet weather.

Pit-a-pat! Pit-a-pat! The branches shook their mimic shower upon my upturned face. A faint mist, like a giant's breath upon a mirror, arose from the still, glassy surface of the pool.

As I stood, drinking in the sweet, moist freshness, the air vibrant all around with the music of a thousand runnels and rillets, a winged ray of light shot from the crumbling grey masonry of the bridge. It was a kingfisher; the iridescent green and azure of its plumage flashed close before my delighted gaze, dipped to the pool, skimmed the whole length of the surface and disappeared in the mist on the farther side.

This is the second time I have seen one here. The last I saw in July, when the water-lilies were out, on a day of almost garish sunlight. To-day, in the watery, blue-grey atmosphere, it showed its brilliant colours far more plainly. Last time I saw one I made enquiries, hoping to hear that it had a regular haunt somewhere within walking distance, but all the information I could gain was that the landlord of the village inn had once shot one, and had it still in a glass case in his bar parlour, and that I ought to call and see it someday when I was "up along", for "'ee'd be ever so pleased to show it 'ee, that 'ee 'ud!"

I never availed myself of this vicarious invitation for I do not think I should care to meet the man who could find it in his heart to slay so much beauty and to keep the stuffed body in an atmosphere of stale beer and bad tobacco . . .

One family of birds, and one alone, is both flocking and nesting this month. In the rookery it is spring already. Every day as I pass beneath the tall wind-tossed elms where their home is I see the nests taking form and increasing. The noise and bustle the birds make over it is simply deafening; they seem never to take a twig or put it in place without a consultation of the whole tribe. But, unlike most great talkers, the rooks are good workers, too, and their rough bundle of twigs will be in place and young birds within it before the hedgerow birds have put straw to straw.

Last year there were young birds in the Peverel rookery by the end of February, and some years they are said to have been earlier still. It may be so from immemorial custom, and Gilbert White may have had this particular settlement in mind when he wrote:

> *"Sooth'd by the genial warmth, the cawing rook*
> *Anticipates the spring"–**

for his own parish of Selborne is only six miles from Peverel; and, standing as this group of tall elms does by the roadside, he must often have passed beneath it.

It is easy to imagine him, the very first of English nature writers, with his powdered hair and sober clerical garb, jogging along the road on his fat grey mare, stopping beneath the elms to gaze upwards at the noisy black birds about their business of nest-making, lingering, perhaps, to jot down a date or caress some early spray of blackthorn with his riding-whip; then jogging homeward away over Peverel, the most sober and modest, yet happiest, of men! . . .

The turn of the year is certainly behind us: a thousand sights, scents, and sounds declare the fact. But exactly at what moment the mystic change took place, and Nature, writing "Finis" to the tale of last year, started without pause Chapter I of this, is a mystery. Officially, I suppose, the turn of the year is at midnight upon the shortest day, when the earth starts spinning the 580-odd million miles yearly trip round the sun again. But Nature knows no calendar; and long before that moment came sap was rising, buds were swelling, and this year's shoots pushing upwards from the soil. Earlier still, the last leaves of last year were thrust from the bough by the rising life of this. So there seems to be no definite beginning: the seasons move in a circle.

Wild life in the countryside shares this new stirring of energy with man; lizards creep out to sun themselves upon the heath; bats flit weakly at night from their dark retreats; hedgehogs prowl round the tree-roots and hedgerows. The smaller birds are flitting in pairs. If one chaffinch or yellowhammer starts from the hedge, another is bound to follow: starlings are busy beneath the eaves with strands of coarse grass. When a cold snap comes the work is only suspended; at the first gleam of sunshine they are out and at it again.

From the hedgerow bushes comes a subdued

---

*In "On the Dark, Still, Warm Weather", *The Natural History of Selborne*.

bubbling and twittering – not the full jubilation of spring, but a kind of tentative murmur of song, as though the small singers knew that winter was not far away, and feared to tempt its return by making too sure.

The skylark knows no such prudence; almost before the rain is over he is up, wings still wet, singing and soaring towards the least rift of blue and silver in the clouds. Half-way up Peverel is a square of open turf where a cottage once stood, and in the air above it one morning this week I counted no less than five skylarks all singing and soaring together.

What particular attraction that square of coarse turf holds for these birds I do not know; but, no matter at what daylight hour it is visited in early spring, there are always larks singing above it. Perhaps the birds which frequent it form a clan, unrelated to the families in the valley below, for every year there are nests cupped beside tuffets of the coarse grass, or tucked away in the ancient hoof-marks of cattle which have grazed there.

The skylark's nest is one of the least skilfully hidden and yet most difficult to find of all nests. It is hopeless to set out deliberately to discover one, for the human being walking through long grass is like a giant walking in a wood, his head above the tree-tops – there is always a veil of green between him and the earth beneath. Apart from that, it is possible to stand and gaze upon a lark's nest and yet not notice it, for both the plumage of the sitting bird and the colour of the eggs when exposed tone so well with the earth tints around that they are practically invisible at a few yards' distance. It is when an intruding footstep startles the mother and she flies up almost underfoot that the nest is disclosed . . .

The sheep-fold is now the scene of much innocent frolic; the lambs, grown larger and stronger, frisk all day in the outer court of their straw and hurdle built house. At the approach of a stranger they back towards their mothers, enquiring the while with innocent eyes if the intruder be friend or foe; then,

deciding that, in any case, it is nearly lunch-time, hide their little black nozzles in the maternal fleece. Sometimes, if the mother is not at hand and the shepherd is, they will accept him as a substitute, pushing their heads into his horny hand and rubbing their small, soft bodies against his mud-stained corduroys.

Shepherd himself is getting a little weary. His frost-blue eyes have rather a strained look, and his walk is more bent than usual. Eight weeks of short sleep are telling upon him at his three-score years and five. Every lambing season, he says, writes one more wrinkle on the shepherd's brow; so his own network is not to be wondered at, for he has seen forty-two such seasons. But he is never too tired or too busy to tell the tale of how, when his father died, he was told to "carry on", until a new shepherd could be hired at the Heath Fair. By the time fair-time came he was doing so well that the hiring of an older man was never mentioned, and he has remained in sole charge ever since. "Still carrying on," as he says . . .

In the wood just now, the air is full of the keen scent of cut bark. They are sawing up and carting the trees which fell in the December gale. There is a sad gap by the gate where the great beech known as "the Grey lady" used to stand. This beech was one of the beauties of the wood, with its massive grey pillar of a trunk and widely spreading boughs. The outer branches were so long they drooped to the earth and enclosed a perfect bower, a green mansion of shade.

Within that circle upon hot summer days the light was subdued to a green gloom. Children who played there in the school holidays called it "the house", and furnished it with chairs and tables constructed of moss and twigs. Sometimes they would arrange pebbles and shards upon the table for cups and plates, and lay a neat "fire" of fir-cones between the root, then leave it so for weeks, like a fairies' house, from which the occupants were abroad and might return at any moment.

Grown-ups found "the house" a useful retreat in a sudden shower, but only up to a certain point; for, although the flat, polished leaves of the beech are the best of those of any tree in keeping off slight rain, they are no use at all in a prolonged downpour. For ten minutes or a quarter of an hour the drops can be heard splashing off the bright surface, but when the rain has had time to collect it forms little waterspouts which come suddenly spurting, first in one place, then in another, seeming to aim at the back of the neck of the would-be shelterer.

They have dragged the trunk and boughs of the beech aside, and only a circle of brown earth, layers deep with husks and leaf-mould, is left to mark the spot where the Grey Lady stood through so many scores of seasons. When spring comes a thousand lush green things will spring in the rich and practically virgin soil, and even the circle cast by its shade will be obliterated . . .

The shepherd . . . conducted me to a spot beneath the hedge where, he said, he had something to show me. It was a very pale and sickly-looking primrose, the very first of the year, and early at that. As he moved away the bracken he had piled around to keep the wind from it, the one poor flower seemed to shiver in its rosette of shrivelled leaves, and I remarked upon its poverty and thinness, saying, rather thoughtlessly, that I preferred each flower in its proper season. He paused in his ministrations, his work-roughened hands – so well-shaped and sensitive-looking for all their disfigurements – trembling with age and eagerness.

"It is *wonderful* for the time of year," I amended hastily.

"Well, there!" he admitted reflectively. "'Tis but a primrose to you, as to most people, a sight you'll see a many more times if you're spared as long as is natural; but when you're gettin' on in years so that each time you see th' like – a wanny, tender thing like that springing straight from th' frosty ground – and know you won't see many more, and *that* perhaps th' last, you seems to set a value on it. It seems to have a sort of meaning somehow, to be something more than a common flower – but there, I couldn't explain it!"

I do not think I was quite as much in favour with the shepherd as usual when I went my way. I had failed to perceive exactly what was in the mind of my friend, and he withdrew into himself, and would talk of nothing more intimate than the weather; but I know that before I pass that way again I shall be forgiven, for, after living seventy years amongst those who cannot once in a hundred times rise with or follow his thoughts, he has learned to accept sympathy with joy, and not to expect comprehension.

The sheltered hedgerow within which the sheepfold has been made is at least a month in advance of others in more exposed positions. Upon the heath, which rises to a brooding hill above it, it is winter still. The morning frosts powder a dark and lifeless world; ice remains upon the pools all day, and the small boys who mind the commoners' cows beat their hands together and long for home and tea-time. But frosts which last all day on the uplands often thaw in the moist and sheltered valley by noon; then, if the mild, winter sun peeps out, the middle of each day is a miniature spring.

Within that warm shelter by the middle of February the hedge seems positively to burn with rising sap; against the warm purple of the hawthorns the honeysuckle puts out adventurous trails of delicate green; hazel-catkins

toss in the wind, and even the more cautious blackthorn shows a pearl at each tip – pearls which may burst into blossoms in a week, or remain as they are for a couple of months, according to the weather.

When closely examined, the earth beneath the hedge is found to be surging with growth, from the mould of the ditch spring strong shoots of wild-arum,

46

dog's-mercury, fool's-parsley, and a hundred other green and growing things; the bindweed forges upward and hurries towards the bush which supported it last year at a rate which befits a plant which has ten or twelve feet to travel. Nor, early as it is, are flowers lacking. The ground-ivy flashes a glimpse of mauve between the upstanding, butter-coloured lamps of the closed celandines; there are dandelions, too, and daisies peep from the wet turf of the field-margin – poor, frail daisies with scarcely a tinge of pink, but most welcome as forerunners of April's shining bands.

Upon a mound of loose earth, thrown up in some excavations, a throng of pale, mealy-golden coltsfoot flowers open to every glimpse of sun. These flowers have a naked look, the tender, scaly, brown-green stems rising from the cold earth without a single leaf to clothe them. The Greeks used to call the coltsfoot "the son before the father", on account of this trait. Later in the spring the bank will be clothed with the broad flat leaves, each with a white downy under-side, and bearing in shape a distant resemblance to the horse's hoof which gives the plant its name.

Blooming as it does without protection at an inclement season, the coltsfoot has developed a curious protective habit. At night, as soon as the upper air becomes colder than the earth, each golden eye turns downward and remains bowed until the air is warmer than the earth again. But, in spite of this shrinking from cold, the coltsfoot is one of the most hardy of flowers, finding a footing in the most waste and desolate places, such as on heaps of slag beside railway lines, on building-plots in towns, or even upon the pavements of those suburbs of the future we see staked out on the outskirts of cities.

The hedgerow is so crammed with interest that it would provide studies for more hours than there are in the day. It is one of the old double hedgerows which, thickened with trees and twined about with creepers, used to be a common feature in English scenery. Such hedgerows used to be, and still are where they have been retained, both gardens for every kind of wild-flower and sanctuaries for birds and the lesser animals. Along the banks, between the double hedges, children have made small, well-defined paths, leading, for those small enough to explore them, to many a secret bower entwined with honeysuckle or wild-hop. Between the roots of the hawthorns the earliest violets are always found, and later in the year there are primroses and bluebells, with nuts and blackberries to follow.

Such hedgerows are gradually disappearing, together with the small, irregularly-shaped fields they bounded. The use of the tractor calls for square, open spaces. The modern, scientific farmer does not approve of such waste of space and harbourage for "vermin". In highly-farmed districts, the old, untidy, picturesque hedgerow is doomed. In districts such as this, where the soil is poor and the farming casual, they may still be seen, the hawthorns and hazels which compose them immemorially old, the lanes which run beneath sunk six or eight feet by the traffic of centuries.

The chief glory of those hedgerows in February is the hazel. Above every lane and along each field-side the catkin tosses, grey in dull weather, gold in sunshine, turning against the dark woods to a greenish smoke. Conspicuous as it is now as the only wild-flower to be gathered in sufficient quantities to furnish us with a nosegay, no one can go for a country walk without noticing it. Most of us greet it with eager joy as the first offering of the year. But, although few observed it, the hazel catkin was with us all the winter. Directly the leaves fell, the stiff upright grey tails appeared. For weeks they stood obstinately still, bare husks without visible life in them; then, as the light increased with the turn of the year, the catkin tails lengthened, turned downward, and prepared to disperse the pollen with which they were charged.

Now they have grown yellow and fluffy, so light and loose that the slightest shake sends the pollen-dust into the air like smoke. The number of spores carried by each tail must be enormous; it would be as easy to number the sands of the sea as the offspring of a single tree. Yet the nuts borne by the same tree can be counted easily; in poor seasons there are none to count, and all February's lavish flinging of gold-dust has been in vain. Given the best of seasons, it is not possible that a millionth part of the pollen-dust can come to anything, for the simple reason that the fruit-bearing flowers of the hazel are not one to a million of the pollen spores.

The fruit-bearing flower of the hazel grows upon the same tree with the pollen-bearing catkin. Although a bright-red in colour, it is so minute that many people pass it by every year of their lives without noticing it. Before it is open the female flower is not easily distinguished from the leaf-bud, which it closely resembles, but once the apex has burst and released the tuft of crimson threads which form the tiny stemless flower, it is plainly visible upon the leafless twigs. When examining the tree for it, the observer cannot fail to be struck by the over-abundance of catkins compared to the number of female flowers. This lavishness is a feature of all wind-fertilised plants, the medium being so casual that, for every pollen-speck which reaches its proper goal, a thousand float away and fall elsewhere . . .

Inherited instinct has taught the birds to make haste slowly. Although St Valentine's Day is the official mating date nesting does not begin for some weeks after. Birds flutter from bush to bush in pairs; starlings carry straws to the roof in their bills; partridges run two and two in the furrows, and even the robin, a lone bird for the last six months, shows a disposition to seek the company of its own kin. But they all seem to know as well as we do ourselves that the mild spells are to be enjoyed, but not trusted to last; and in spite of a few early nests reported from different parts of the country each year the main movement in the building line does not commence in a normal season until February is out.

That month is devoted to the donning of spring plumage, the choosing of mates, disposing of rivals, and settling of plans. Already many of the male birds are in fine feather, the pink waistcoat of the chaffinch flushed to a pale flame, the robin's crimson and bronze more cheerful than ever, the blackbird's glossy coat sleeked to the jetty blackness which so well sets off the brightness of his orange-tawny bill. The starling is the most completely transformed of all. A month ago he was dark and draggled, haunting the doorstep for crumbs and opening and shutting his beak with a melancholy "Chap! Chap!" of self-pity; now he is a gay fellow in his smart coat of many lustres, and has so far forgotten past favours as to tweak at and destroy each crocus bud as it opens.

Quite contrary to human usage all that is brightest and best in apparel is strictly reserved for the male sex, and the female bird has to be content with a little extra burnish on her quiet brown or grey. There is, however, no need for her to add to her attractions by means of dress, for she is the sought-for and choosing side to a match, and the rivalry between her suitors is already bound to be sufficiently keen.

Every sunny hour now sees the comedy of a wooing played out, the rival suitors preening and bowing before their chosen lady, puffing out their breast-feathers and stretching their wings as though to show all their points off to the best advantage. While they decide which is the more worthy of her graces, she hops from bough to bough, or pecks delicately at a clod, with an air of real or assumed indifference; then, the question decided in some mysterious manner between the three of them, meekly follows the victor, an obedient little wife . . .

Upon Christmas morning a nut-hatch appeared at my birds' breakfast table, hustling among the garden birds to claim more than his share of the suet, and then expressing his thanks in an acrobatic display, running upside-down about the tree-trunks and dangling precariously upon the coconut hung at the end of a string for the tits. As long as it remained above-head it was graceful enough in its movements, but upon the ground, among the garden birds, it had a heavy, clumsy appearance, due, no doubt, to its large head in contrast with its short tail. These features, together with its bright plumage, in which blue and a beautiful pale orange predominate, give it a strange, un-English appearance which has even at times caused it to be mistaken for a parrot.

Still more strikingly un-English-looking is the solitary heron which has haunted the streams and pools about Peverel this winter. This morning it stood for over an hour, up to its knees in water, fishing a pool in one of the curves of the stream. Against the background of tall reeds, with the red stems of pine-trees towering above, the quaint, stork-shaped bird, with its long legs and crested head, would have made a perfect study for a Japanese print. For moments together it stood perfectly motionless, its eyes intent upon the water; then, with a sudden dart forward, it would spike some small fish upon its long bill and swallow it whole.

It is seldom one of these birds appears in the neighbourhood, for the nearest heronry is seven or eight miles distant; but in winter the heron leaves its community, and, touring the country, forages for itself, and if, in the course of its travels, it finds a spot where the fishing is good, it will return to it again and again, keeping the knowledge of its discovery to itself, exactly as some human anglers will do. It is one of the most successful of fishers, for its patience is unlimited and its eyesight keen. Small fish it swallows whole; larger ones are quickly negotiated and gulped down, while if fish fail, a frog makes a change of diet, or a water rat may be sighted and its skull split with one stroke of that strong, merciless bill.

About the middle of this month the birds return to their ancient haunts. The heronry from which this one probably came has been established from time immemorial. It is situated in the tops of some very old beeches which surround a small lake in one of the last uncleared remnants of a royal forest. There, high in the leafy boughs, so far overhead that one might pass beneath a dozen times without noticing them, the large, flat nests of twigs and dry grass make a kind of platform running from tree to tree.

Those who rest beside the lake in summer are often startled by a loud clapping of wings and giving of boughs as one of the large, strange-looking birds takes to the air with the peculiarly buoyant, tossing motion due to its lightness of body. "Like a moll-hern, all legs and wings", used to be the country-man's description of anything of deceptive appearance, from an overgrown boy to a cabbage with no heart in it – not a bad simile, considering that the heron measures over four feet across its wings, and yet weighs only a little over three pounds.

What becomes of each generation of young herons is a mystery, for the colonies grow no larger with new nests, nor do new settlements appear to be made. Like a rookery, but even more so, a heronry is a cherished feature of a country estate, and many a newly-established landowner would pay a large sum of money if it were possible to transfer one to his new demesne. Most of those already in existence have been known upon their present sites for centuries, neither increasing nor decreasing in size, although a second clutch of three or four pale green eggs is often deposited in a nest before the first family is fledged. Some of the young birds fall a prey to hawks, but the heron, though a large bird and a good mark, is a lightweight, and often gets the better of its pursuer by soaring above it; others are shot by the curious, though not so many as formerly, for country people are better informed than those of a generation ago and no longer point a gun as a matter of course at anything unusual. Making allowance for every likely accident, every community ought, at least, to double its numbers each year.

Yet, instead of forming fresh colonies, the heron is disappearing from some districts. Here and there about the country a deserted heronry may be seen, a thickening of twigs in the upper boughs of tall old pines or beeches, nothing for the eye of the casual observer to rest on, but to the nature-discoverer a bird-city of the past . . .

Last night we had one of those wondrous sunsets only to be seen in open downland country. For a quarter of an hour the west was a blaze of gold and crimson and amethyst; then, as the sun dropped behind the thin, dark line of the distant hills, the craggy cloud-masses broke into a fleece of floating purple, and the whole sky was diffused with a rose-coloured glow.

"A red night is the shepherd's delight," quoted one, and we all made sure of a fine day to follow. But, in spite of the old weather tag, this morning broke grey and dripping, and the shepherd descending from his night-long vigil in the lambing-fold had an old sack draped about his shoulders to keep off the rain.

An hour later, in dry clothes and cheered by a good breakfast, he passed on his way back to relieve the underling he had left in charge.

"Why did it rain after such a sunset? 'Cos the rain wer' there, and had to come down, I guess! Couldn't you see it piled up in them girt clouds? Very fine they looked for a while, I'll allow, all red and yellery, but before and after they wer's black as my hat!"

"So *you* were not deceived by the red night?"

He laughed and good-temperedly.

"It's always safe to foretell rain in February, so no credit to me for that; but, as a matter o' fact, I wer' a bit suspicious of all them fireworks in the sky last night. Then all day yesterday I 'eard th' trains rush out o' th' tunnel a good three miles away, and that, as you know, means a wet 'un; not to mention the wet wind as sprung up about midnight. You could smell rain and taste rain for hours before it begun."

"Then the red night means nothing?"

"Oh, I wouldn't go so far's to say that; but the shepherd's red night is a different thing to yon – just a red flag on a grey sky as like as not. As to th' shepherd's delight! Not much doin' in that way at this time o' year, what with workin' th' clock round six nights out o' seven. Hark to 'em! Cryin' for me to come back along like a lot o' babbies callin' f ther mothers," and he hobbled off in the direction from which the thin waiting cries of young lambs came floating on the wet wind.

Later in the morning I watched him among them, grinding out the sweet, creamy pulp of turnips for the ewes and shaking out warm dry straw for their beds, pausing now and again to take a look into one of the hurdled-in enclosures where the invalids lay with patient, pain-dimmed eyes; or to pick up some woolly adventurer whose brand-new legs had given out upon its first walk beyond the shelter of the straw-padded hurdles.

A shepherd's life is a hard one and ill-paid, counting by modern money standards; for him there is no eight or any other hour day. As long as one member of his flock needs his care he must stay with it, must at all times work from dawn to dusk; but, though he complains bitterly at times of the hardships of his lot, I do not think our shepherd would change it for one of pensioned ease.

For one thing, as long as he remains in office, a shepherd is a man of some importance upon a farm. No one can take up his work without training as they might that of an ordinary labourer.

There used to be an old country saying: "Not every man is a shepherd who carries a crook." A whole lifetime is not too long for a shepherd to learn his trade in. Not only must he know all about the different breeds of sheep, which thrive best upon different soils, and the proper food and treatment for each, but he must at times turn surgeon and nurse as well as guardian.

This man, as I have said, thinks nothing of sitting up night after night with his ewes, sometimes nearly distracted by the number and complexity of his "cases", at others merely watching and waiting, with only the gentle breathing of his charges, the soughing of the wind in the elm-tops and the marching of the stars for company. No wonder the earliest astronomers were shepherds! After twenty, thirty, or even forty years in the open at all hours of the day and night the face of the heavens must become as an open book . . .

Until recently, as perhaps still in some parts, it was the custom as soon as

the young birds were fledged and learning to fly for the choice spirits of the place from forge and field and village alehouse to gather beneath the rookery trees for a morning's sport. Those who had guns and were licensed to use them shot openly; others waited their turn for a furtive loan of a gun, or did a little on their own account with slings and stones. A little betting was done and a great deal of beer consumed, and the result was a limp and mangled heap of feathered corpses, of which only the legs and wings were usable for the rook pie which was the ostensible object of the massacre.

The scene upon such an occasion would be well worth describing, for some fine old crusted country characters were present, and rustic wit and rustic anecdote flowed freely in a dialect now seldom heard. There was the rookery, too, in all the cold purity of an early spring morning, celandines opening, buds bursting and branches swaying in the wind. But the main impression left upon the mind of a child was of tragedy.

It was like the sacking of a city. At one moment the quiet earth and the cheerful bustle of breakfast-time in the tree-tops. Then the onslaught, so sudden, so overwhelming. As long as the shooting was going on the parent birds would circle around in the sky, uttering the most pitiful lamentations as their helpless babes were shot down under their gaze, and the moment the terror was over they went back to feed and comfort the few survivors left in the nests.

Like those of many other birds and animals, the reputation of the rook has improved with the extension of knowledge. Until a very few years ago the noisy black-coated rogue was looked upon as one of the worst of farm pests; a reputation not altogether unfounded, for a school of rooks will clear a field of newly-planted seed-corn if once they set about it.

But even the rook is not quite so black as he has been painted. He is now credited also with his depredations amongst the eggs and grubs of the insect pests which cause the farmer a thousand times more loss and vexation than the rook himself does.

March

March

WHAT A LOVELY flower the snowdrop is, so pure and cold outwardly, yet "all beautiful within" with green and gold. It is one of the most generally beloved of all flowers, too, for it appeals to everybody: to the artistic by the grace of its own loveliness, and to the average nature as the harbinger of spring.

It is not often found growing wild in Hampshire: even those I saw to-day, though growing for centuries untended, are probably of garden origin; for somewhere, quite close to the spot where they grow, one of the Angevin kings had a hunting lodge, and in one of his household account-books may still be seen the entry of a charge for "Maken a lytel plesaunce for the Queen's Majesty".

The royal dwelling has disappeared – even the foundation stones have vanished.* The deer and wild boar, so stringently preserved for the king's sport, are as extinct as the wolves which came before them and gave their name to the district; but it is quite likely that all through the centuries, while thrones have rocked and palaces been overturned, these tender and fragile flowers have spread and overflowed and flourished until the few roots planted

*Linchborough Lodge, near Conford, reputedly stood on the site of a hunting lodge built for Edward I. It has recently been razed, but the snowdrops still remain. The land around it is now part of Longmoor Ranges, and access is forbidden when red flags are flying.

in the queen's little garden have become a snowy mantle for the whole hillside . . .

March is a month of broad effects, of firm outline and clear colour. Blue skies are blue, indeed; green fields clear as emerald, and the road, newly dried by wind and sun, runs, a pale sand-coloured streak, straight up and over the hill-top towards infinity.

This morning I passed an upland pasture, a pale green slope running up between leafless woods to where a belt of pines filtered the windy blue of the sky through their scanty boughs. Into this field had been turned the sheep and lambs from the lambing-pen and they grouped themselves in quaintly regular circles round the turnip heaps the farm cart had shot down at intervals for them to feed on.

But there were other good judges of a fine juicy turnip abroad. The rooks, drifting in twos and threes across the sky, spied the feast from above and flapped down to claim a share. Soon there were more rooks than sheep in the field. They strutted, glossy black and shining, up and down the pale green of the slope. Some, as they grew bolder, perched upon the backs, necks, and even the heads of their gentle hostesses; or, alighting, took possession, with many pecks and raucous cries, of the root heaps, until the inoffensive sheep drew back, and the little lambs, not yet promoted to such substantial fare, formed small groups of their own and gazed in innocent-eyed wonder at the strange black coats and bad table-manners of the noisy invaders . . .

New life is everywhere. At every sunny angle of the hedgerows the buds are bursting into a light veil of green; new grass springs in the meadows, fresh rushes beside the stream; things in the garden move so quickly one can almost "see them grow". The grass-margin beneath the roadside hedge is a garden set with a thousand tiny, unconsidered wild things, speedwell and wild forget-me-not and the meek, innocent-looking star-of-Bethlehem. Farther down, from the moisture of the ditch, springs the strong lush green of the cuckoo-pint. Soon the children will be searching the long, broad, lily-of-the-valley shaped leaves for "lords and ladies", as they call the fleshy pointing finger the plant puts out in spring.

These fleshy, pale red or cream-coloured spikes are not the true flower, but only an insect-attracting device to secure fertilisation. The real flower clusters round the base of the spoke, a mere dusting of infinitesimal mealy-coloured florets. As soon as the seed is set, spike and leaf alike die down and the whole plant vanishes to reappear later in the year as a cluster of brilliant orange-scarlet berries at the tip of a single stalk. Not one observer in a hundred connects these bright, evil-looking berries with the cuckoo-pint of spring. In Hampshire they are known simply as "poison-berries", and no country child will lay so much as a finger upon them.

They *are* highly poisonous; but, then, so are the leaf and spike as well. So it would be interesting, if it were possible, to trace back to its source this superstitious shrinking from the berries only. Perhaps some bold experimenter, some Ancient Briton, or man of the Stone Age, partook of the tempting-looking fruit and perished, and through the centuries his fate has faded from memory to tradition, and from tradition to instinctive repulsion.

Another flower of the March hedgerows, and one of which nothing but good can be said, is that little golden flower, with rays like the rising sun, the lesser celandine. Always the very earliest of our wild flowers to appear, this bright, cheerful little thing was with us this year by the middle of January. Ever since it has gone on blooming and spreading, opening its golden discs to every gleam of the winter sun, and twirling itself up to a tiny twist of ashen yellow in rain and cold.

Coming as this flower does when all the earth is bare and brown, and the snowdrop in the garden and its own cheerful gold upon the roadside without are the only visible signs of the better time coming, one might expect it would be eagerly watched for and welcomed with enthusiasm. Not so. The majority of people tread it underfoot without seeing it at all; the country folk even deny it a name of its own, and lump it with the buttercups, an entirely different family.

"How bright and cheerful the celandines are!" I ventured to the woman at whose cottage I was buying eggs last month.

"Oh, them!" she said vaguely, when, in answer to her uncomprehending look, I pointed to a whole flood of living sunshine upon the bank by her gateway. "Don't know as I've ever noticed 'em before!"

I concealed my astonishment, for country people hate to appear behind-hand with strangers in nature knowledge: but I could not help thinking that one regardless of such largess at her gate in the gloom of winter must be blind indeed . . .

How vain is prophecy! At the very moment I foretold in my last month's paper that no bird would build upon Peverel before February was out, a pair of starlings had a nest already completed beneath the eaves of the very roof I was writing under. A few days later a choked water-spout brought to light the rough bundle of dried grass which is all the starling family consider necessary in the way of a nest.

It was a pleasant sign of the times that the young man who was working upon the roof took the trouble to climb down the ladder to find out my wishes about it, and afterwards took infinite trouble to turn the water aside to spare it and the three pale greenish-blue eggs it contained. A workman of an older generation would have demolished it as a matter of course; but, thanks to the nature study in schools now, the love of, and sympathy with, all living creatures is becoming universal.

The workman, although such a practical friend to that particular pair, did not scruple to criticise the habits of their family. "Awkward things, starlings, to have about a garden in the cheery season," he declared, and added that a regular flock of them came from "all over" every year when his father's Mayduke tree was ripe, and stripped it "as clean as a whistle!"

They certainly are rather a nuisance from a gardener's point of view. Even I, loving birds better than gardens on the whole, cannot help wishing sometimes that they would pay for the free run of the ripe fruit later by leaving the spring buds alone. This week I am continually running from my desk by the window to chase them away from the crocus beds; but no sooner am I back than I see them again, tugging and pulling at the leaves until the white thready portion near the bulb is exposed, and tearing the petals until they lie, like shreds of mauve and yellow ribbon, about the lawn.

Yet, annoying as these depredations are, I would not be without the perpetrators, for the starling is one of the quaintest and most lovable of birds. In wet weather, when other birds crouch beneath the boughs for shelter, he is at his best and brightest, shuffling up and down in his fine spring suit, a metallic black, shot with purple and green and picked out with pearl; darting his yellow bill into the soft wet earth for larvae or wireworm, varying his harsh but cheerful chuckle with a kind of piping whistle, as though to signal to some overhead passerby that both wireworms and crocuses were excellent upon Peverel, so why go farther and fare worse? . . .

Last night a long white "mare's tail" parted the dun clouds, and the sunset was a dull brass-coloured streak upon the horizon. The shepherd, driving stakes to enclose a fresh square of turnip-greens for his flock, called out to me as I passed.

"Better get plenty wood and water indoors," he advised; "that 'oss's tail over the trees means 'weather'. We shall see wind and rain before we see sun again, and under cover'll be the best place for such as can keep there."

My protestation that I loved "weather" fell flat. He dreads wind and rain so much for his ewes that he can never be persuaded that they are less harmful for others of their sex; and, though he has seen me out in a storm a score of times, he still persists in the belief that my one great fear is of wetting my feet.

The storm came on before many hours had gone, and all night my cottage bedroom was a small enclosed silence in the midst of turmoil. Wind and rain beat in spasmodic gusts upon roof and window; water gurgled from the gutters; garden tree-tops strained and roared, and from across the moors came the hoarse *drub, drub,* of the winds of March.

There is something disturbing and exciting in such sounds, especially at night. The mind refuses to rest, even while the body drowses, and visualises, like a series of pictures, the dark outer world, following the wind across wet heath and glinting water over the solid hills to the heaving, storm-tossed sea.

Between sleeping and waking, towns, farms, and villages are seen, all hushed in the tranquility of a perfect trust in Nature's moods; soft, brown-furred animals, curled up in their homes in the sandy soil; birds rocking upon storm-tossed boughs; fish in the soft mud of pools; insects in hive and clod – all

living things nestling closer to the bosom of earth as the great winds rush at who knows how many miles a minute across her face . . .

Upon Saturdays and Sundays now the children here go "violeting", straggling along the hedgerows, searching the leaves, and hailing each discovery with shouts of joy. The purple violets are the most prized, for they are scarce, the white variety for some reason or other being far more abundant here. These white wild violets are very frail, and wilt in the hand like snowdrifts in the sun, so what the children do with them I do not know. Upon the stalk they are delicately lovely. Upon a field margin between here and the village to-day I came upon a long patch of them in bloom, like exquisite small shells upon a green beach.

The field where they grew was billowy with autumn-sown wheat, blackthorn blew in the hedges, the sky was radiant above, a few yards away were dark heath and leafless woods, but in that one sunny spot it was fully spring. So warm and drying was the sun that the footpath which cuts the field in halves, straight up the slope, was already yellow with dust.

This path, which leads to nowhere in particular – merely up the hill, through a little wood, and out upon the heath again – might easily be dispensed with; for it is a sore annoyance to the ploughman, who either has to turn or lift his plough bodily over each time he comes to it in the course of his furrow. But it is an ancient right of way, and when, a few years ago, an attempt was made to close it, the whole population of the heath assembled one Sunday after church, broke down the barriers, and trampled the corn. Since then it has become a favourite walk: children going to school and men to their work assert their ancient right by going a little out of their way to use it.

The attempt to close such a footpath is very rare here. About Peverel, for the most part, all well-conducted ramblers are at liberty to go where they will. It is upon the large game-preserving estates beyond the Sussex border that liberty is restricted. There, in the woods, the gamekeeper seems to lie constantly in wait, and long and bitter are the arguments between him and trespassers of spirit. It is vain to insinuate to him that for one man to lay claim to a primrose wood or a bluebell dell and to pay another man to watch it is an outrage upon the rest of humanity, because he has been brought up in the belief that the "estate" is simply so many acres of shelter for game birds, and that it is as criminal for an outsider to stray there to pick primroses as it would be for him to walk into a neighbour's garden to steal cabbages. His talk of "a summons" is an empty threat, for there is no penalty for trespass unless some damage is done, such as breaking down a fence or cutting trees; but, for the sake of one's own self-respect, it is better to keep to the public ways than to run the risk of discomfiture.

As I climbed the sloping field-path to pick blackthorn sprays for my vases, a couple of hares tumbled from the green corn a few yards from my feet. At any other time of year they would have sensed me and kept out of sight, but this is the month when the hare proverbially goes mad, and, if the behaviour of that particular pair was typical, the proverb is well founded. For several minutes they rolled, and bit, and butted, first one uppermost, then the other; finally, they both sat on their haunches and fought a regular pitched battle with their front paws.

Such absolute absorption in their own affairs as not to see or hear an on-looker so near to them is exceptional; but from a distance such scenes are one of the features of March. Once, by moonlight upon a hillock on the Downs, I saw a party of four or five of them in silhouette, chasing each other round and round, bucking and leaping, as though they had met for a concerted game.

The hare is often confused by town-dwellers with the much commoner rabbit; but it is not only a larger, but a wilder and more beautiful animal. Seen at close quarters against a background of green, its sandy coat, unmixed with grey, is almost golden. Its long sensitive ears, dark, pleading eyes, and figure the very incarnation of swift grace make it one of the most beautiful, as well as the wildest and shyest, of English wild animals.

It is well for the young leveret that it does not come into the world naked and helpless, as the young of the rabbit does; for the hare has no safe, warm burrow under ground to deposit its young in, but makes its nursery upon the bare earth with only a tuffet of grass or a clump of bracken to shelter it. From this "form", as it is called, the young leverets are taught to scatter at the approach of danger. Sometimes, if the danger is sudden and close at hand, they will trust, as their parents do, to their protective colouring, and crouch motionless against the sandy earth until the intruder has passed on.

In such cases a hare will allow a human being to come within a few feet of it, or even to walk round it. By averting the eyes and walking very leisurely and unconcernedly, it is quite easy to persuade any wild creature that it is unnoticed, but the hare is more than ordinarily confident. As a child, I once witnessed the taking of one through this trait. My brother and I were playing "light-houses"

upon the top of a hayrick in the corner of a small ploughed field. By a footpath across the same field a number of farm labourers were going home from their work, smoking and chatting as they went, with the low, dazzling sun in their eyes. As they shambled on, the foremost of them started a large hare from the grassy pathway. A cry of "Tally ho!" was soon raised, and one of the men, a little more active than his fellows, started in pursuit.

"Better keep y'r breath to blow y'r taters," his mates called after him derisively; but he was away and across the field, soon outdistanced, of course, by his quarry.

His chase must have been inspired by some primitive sporting instinct; for, had the rick not come in the way, he might just as well have followed the wind. The hare fled one way round the rick; the man, hoping to cut it off, took the opposite direction, but when he had circled it and came out on the sunny side again the hare had completely disappeared. The hunter stood, his hand shading his eyes, scanning the furrows for a clue, while his mates, with many a jeer at his folly, passed on towards home. He lingered, pretending to light his pipe, until the last of them crossed the stile into the next field; then, taking off his coat and spreading it upon his arm, he proceeded leisurely over the ploughing in the opposite direction to that in which the path lay.

Partly buried in the hay, we children had escaped notice, and were about to resume our game when we saw the man suddenly throw himself sideways to the earth, his coat outspread. The poor hare had trusted too well to its protective colouring; experienced eyes had detected it, squatting earth-coloured upon the sandy earth, for all the dazzling brilliancy of the sunset light.

A great scuffling and struggling ensued, from which the man emerged with a dead hare wrapped in his coat, to be buried in the hay for removal after dark. The whole scene had only taken a few minutes, and he was off across the field, whistling as though nothing had happened, and calling to his mates not to be in "such a deuce of an 'urry", before the thin wailing cries of the hare, so strangely human, had ceased to echo in our horrified ears.

Very sad, of course, that a seemingly respectable workman should be a secret poacher! But, with wages at twelve shillings a week, and six or eight mouths to feed, I think that, after this lapse of time, we may hope that, although out of season, the hare made a savoury stew . . .*

In the water-meadow next to the lambs' leaping place the banks of the stream are a tangle of sallow bushes. A week ago they were studded with silvery-grey catkins, but the warmth of the last few days had drawn the hidden stamens forth, and the silver is feathered over with gold. In the sunny sheltered bend of the stream these flowers make a premature summer for the honey-bees, and all day long such a humming and booming goes on that the passer-by might well think that an early swarm had alighted.

---

*Compare the account of this event in *Lark Rise*, chapter IX.

Where all the myriads of bees come from is a mystery; for, since the Isle of Wight disease swept out hives a few years ago, this has not been a bee-keeping district. Perhaps the scent of the sallow-catkins draws them, for it is one of the most delightfully fragrant in nature, with warmth as well as sweetness in it, and that, and the bright gold of the anthers, seem to gather up the sunshine and to express the very quintessence of it.

These golden-fledged catkins are the male, or pollen-bearing, flowers; the female, or fruit-bearing, ones remain silvery. The two kinds, unlike those of the hazel, grow upon different trees, often yards apart; therefore to trust to the wind for fertilization would be too risky. So some signal, too subtle for our human senses to perceive, is broadcast, and the bees arrive from every point of the compass to gather the nectar to make bee-bread and to carry the pollen to the waiting flowers in return.

The yellow sallow-catkin, with its warm perfume, was the "palm" of the country children of a generation back. In the time of my own childhood it was carried to church on Palm Sunday, accompanied, oddly enough, by dried figs wrapped in blue sugar-paper. Perhaps in some counties the old custom survives, but in this part it seems to be forgotten...

A little farther down stream than the violet island a noisy domestic discussion was taking place. A mallard, magnificently attired in his iridescent spring plumage, had brought his homely little brown wife to prospect for a nesting site. His own taste apparently inclined to a tuft of reeds set round with brambles which a pool cut off more or less from the mainland, and with much noise and many a sly peck, he was trying to shepherd the lady of his choice towards it. Perhaps she considered the spot too isolated, for even a wild duck is not so wild but it likes to quack the time of day to a neighbour; or it may have been that a difference of opinion as to the state of the ground caused the dissension; but for one reason or another the place did not meet with her approval at all, and, just as I came up, matters were coming to a climax.

Acting quite contrary to tradition, the gentleman did all the talking. Time after time he advanced his long strings of arguments in a loud and threatening staccato; and each time, just as he grew heated, the lady turned her back and marched mutely away.

This was too much for him of the dominant sex, and the whole affair ended in something very much like a fight. I left them sulking: one bird upon the bank pretending to be asleep, the other paddling in shallow water. But evidently all came right in the end, for afterwards they sailed amicably past me downstream together, peering into the banks as they passed, as though in search of the ideal spot which would please both.

I should have liked to follow in the hope of ascertaining their final choice,

but just at that moment an apparition appeared which put the wild duck out of my mind. The kingfisher, for it was a kingfisher, flashed rather than flew downstream, a gleam of intense colour, neither dipping nor soaring. As it kept to the course of the water, and the reach was fairly long there, I must have had it in sight for a distance of twenty to thirty yards; but, between its swiftness and my own bewildered delight, it seemed to pass in a flash of blue.

I once heard of a schoolmistress who asked her class if any of them had ever seen a kingfisher. Most of the girls answered "No" at once, but one who did not like to appear ignorant said that she thought she had, but was not quite sure.

"Then you have never seen a kingfisher," decided the mistress. "If you had, you would be quite sure of it!"

I agree with the mistress. No one could ever forget seeing a kingfisher. The colouring is, of course, the most remarkable feature, but the short-tailed, rather top-heavy looking body is also entirely unlike that of any other English bird.

As to the blue of its back and wings, neither gem, flower, nor the plumage of any other bird can match it. It is a shade between blue and green which no device of art or artifice can emulate; painters have attempted it to their own despair, and the "kingfisher blue" of the dyer is a sad travesty. Tennyson called the kingfisher "the sea-blue bird of March," and even that was poetic licence, for, though once or twice in a lifetime a faint reflection of its tint may be seen in sea-water, the translucent blues and greens of the sea are pale compared to the lustre of a kingfisher's wing. It is a living light rather than a colour.

I have never seen a kingfisher's nest; never even met anyone who had a friend who had a friend who had seen one, so I cannot describe it from first,

second, or even third hand experience. In former times the nesting of the kingfisher, or the halcyon, as it was called then, was supposed to be one of the romances of nature. About Christmas time the hen was believed to put out to sea on her nest, as on a raft, and during the time of her incubating such a tranquillising spell was exercised that the very wind and waters were stilled.

Modern naturalists, following Truth even more assiduously than Beauty, and often finding them one at the end of the pursuit, have tracked the kingfisher to its real home, and given us facts instead of poetry. They tell us the bird makes its home underground, usually in the banks of the stream which forms its fishing-ground. A neat oval opening leads into a tunnel two or more feet long, and that, in turn, leads into a circular nesting-chamber, where the pure white eggs repose on a bed of disgorged fish-bones.

It is not difficult to account for this secret underground home, for the brilliant colours of the hen brooding on a nest in the open would expose her and her young to all sorts of dangers; but, none the less, it is a striking thought that the flash of gem-like light we call a kingfisher should be bred in darkness! . . .

We all know the harsh squall of the sparrow of the pavements, but comparatively few are familiar with the gentle little song of a few sweet notes which the hedge-sparrow repeats over and over to itself when it thinks it is unobserved. This little song of the modest grey bird proclaims its relationship to the warbler family. Soon its kindred will be back from overseas – the chiff-chaff, willow-wren, whitethroat, and all the others, including that queen

68

of all warblers, the nightingale – and in their exquisite chorus the gentle voice of this humble relative which has remained with us all the winter will pass unnoticed; but in the meantime the sweet little strain, breathed out in a world of breaking hawthorn buds, is capable of giving much pleasure to the quiet listener.

Simultaneously with the arrival of the chiff-chaff, the whole countryside will break into leaf. The trees, as yet leafless, are thick already with buds, each cluster of future green folded in its sheath of shining brown. Hedges and bushes are farther advanced. Hawthorn, honeysuckle, and wild-rose briar make a young green mist of many shades. The ditches are green with cow-parsley, dog's-mercury, and the upstanding shoots of the climbing things: convolvulus, wild-hop, and the two bryonies. Hidden in this newly-sprung verdure are already flowers for the searcher, the earliest violets, small and short-stemmed, but indescribably sweet; primroses and stitchwort, and sheets of mauve ground-ivy.

Against the pale skies of March the tops of the elms stand out a deep crimson – a flush in this case not wholly due to rising sap, as in some other trees at this time of year, but to the myriad of tiny elm-flowers now in full bloom. Though one of the most obscure of spring flowers, being so minute and growing so high overhead that only one passer-by in a thousand is likely to notice that the tree is in bloom, the flower of the elm is exquisitely coloured and perfectly planned to serve its own purpose. Each bloom consists of an open cup of five reddish stamens, with a forked pistil standing erect in the middle, and it is upon the slightly viscid tips of this fork the pollen, wafted hither and thither by the wind, is caught, and so conveyed to the waiting ovary below . . .

What an essentially English tree the yew is, whether seen, as here, in some ancient churchyard, carved into quaint shapes of walls and arbours and fabulous birds and beasts in some historic garden, or in its wild native state upon the Downs.

Perhaps it is seen at its best in the latter setting. All about the South Downs it grows lavishly, its red stems and glossy dark foliage striking a rare note of colour against the pale turf and pearly chalk-tints of the hills, where even the skies have a paler blue and the clouds are more snowy than elsewhere.

Some of these wild yews of the hills must be tremendously old; not that they ever attain the girth of trunk or circumference of shade they have been known to do in more sheltered positions, but the gnarled toughness of the stems, six or eight twined together to form a trunk, and the grotesque, wind-tortured boughs, all bending one way from the sea, bear the plain impress of centuries.

A thousand years is but an ordinary span of life to the yew. After it has once made its first ten or twelve feet of fairly rapid growth, no man can ever live long enough to see much change in it, and in passing under any tree of apparent old age we may be sure it stood much as it does now in Elizabethan days. English bowmen cut their bows for the Wars of the Roses from still living yews, and who can tell what changes the younger trees we look upon may see in the course of their future centuries...

As sweet as the flowers, and almost flower-like in their bright translucence, are the countless thousands of leaf-buds in March. Bronze buds swelling upon the oak, glistening scaly brown upon the chestnut; ruby buds upon the lime; emerald buds upon the larch; red, green and golden buds in the garden – all hastening to break into the foliage of a new year. They fill the air with a scent which is a savour rather than a perfume, a fresh and wholesome smell which seems the very breath of March.

Perhaps the most beautiful bud of all, and certainly the most delicious of scent, is that of the larch. From my window I can see one tall larch tree standing alone against a background of dark pinewood. A week ago the drooping twigs hung seemingly lifeless as cords, and much the same colour and texture; but to-day every inch is hung with silken tassels of bright jade, and the whole tree stands against the surrounding darkness like a fountain of green flame. In a fortnight or so the green will be studded with soft, rose-coloured rosettes of bloom, and the air for yards around will be sweet with the resinous incense of larch-scent.

Few who did not know the tree intimately would imagine that these "rosy plumelets of the larch", as Tennyson called them, could ever harden into the scaly, varnished wooden objects we know as "pine cones"; but as they mature they lose their colour and their satiny softness, their scales gape to allow the seeds within to be fertilised, and finally they petrify into the cones we find so useful for our winter fires. Even after the winged seeds have been set free the cones still hang on the tree, often side by side with those of other years, and, though every gale scatters a certain number, the tree is never destitute.

Down in the meadow, by the stream, March shows only its sunny side. It is a pleasant spot, a little kingdom, far removed from streets, or even roads; protected from the wind by overhanging woods, beloved of the sun, with its own climate, and full of its own scents and sounds.

This morning to this sheltered sun-trap scores of honey bees had come to take toll of the sallows. The sound of their humming and the murmur of the stream made a tender undertone for the clear, ringing bird-notes, while from farther away came the sighing of tree-tops and the cooing of wild pigeons in the wood.

Along the bank of the stream the sallow bushes, already decorated for Palm Sunday, gleamed silvery with catkins against the March sky; king-cups opened upon the margin of the clear, bright water, and celandines starred the lush green among the willow roots.

Unlike the hazel catkins of last month, those of the sallow are not lightly suspended to swing freely in any gust of air, but stand firm and upright, as they can well afford to do, being independent of the wind for their fertilisation. This week the golden anthers are beginning to appear upon the male flowers, which until recently were as silvery grey as their sisters, fledging the solid-looking little tufts with feathery gold, and furnishing a rich feast of nectar for the bees.

Raised on a dais of turf at a bend in the stream stands an aged yew, and against its thick mass of sombre foliage the slender sallows stand out like snow. But spring has come to the yew of a thousand years as well as to the infant sallows, and the dark, evergreen boughs are powdered with masses of golden-brown florets, from which the bees sip just as freely as they do from the willow anthers.

Farther up the slope, beneath the meadow hedgerow, the strong, lush, arum-like leaves of the cuckoo-pint strike quite a tropical note of luxuriance. Soon the children will be searching the broad, shining leaves for "Lords and Ladies", as they call those flesh-coloured, finger-like spikes which poor mad Ophelia wove into her garland.

"Dead men's fingers" they were called in those days, and the name fits them well, for their cream and pink is clammy to the touch and shot with an ashen purple.

These flashy spikes of the wild arum are neither flower nor fruit, but merely a device to secure fertilisation for the true flower, which lurks, an insignificant mass of mealy florets, at the base. As soon as the seed is set, flower and leaf alike vanish, to reappear in later summer as a cluster of bright orange-scarlet berries at the top of a single stalk.

Along the hedgerows and in the isolated thorn bushes upon the heath the great building movement of the birds is rapidly advancing. Undeterred by cold winds or overcast skies, they fly hither and thither with straws, mud, wool or moss, according to their system of architecture and the available supply. Sometimes, when they realise they are being watched, they will exercise a pretty cunning, entering their hedge or bush by another door as it were, and flitting along the hedgeroots for yards until they come to their chosen spot.

A few of the nests are complete, and have one or more eggs in them; others are at almost every stage, from the first foundation of twigs or straw to the final finishing touches of the lining. Feathers or scraps of down shaken out of doors from the bedding disappear now as if by magic. The leaking pillow or worn eider-down quilt may be a nuisance to the housewife, but it is a blessing to the birds. The chaffinches are especially eager to secure such windfalls, for their nests are, of all those of our most familiar birds, the most exquisitely constructed and softly lined.

The yellowhammer scorns such luxury; just a bunch of coarse grass, with a lining of horse-hair, suffices it for a home. It does not bother much as to construction, either, but lumps its materials together in an untidy mass, rounded and fairly neat within, but shapeless and straggling outwardly.

A pair of these birds have built this year in a kind of cup formed by the decaying surface of a long-felled elm stump, with only a few bramble trails to hide it from the common gaze. True, it is not quite so obvious as it sounds, for the yellow wings of the hen bird, the ragged straw-coloured nest, and the brownish gold of decaying wood all tone together; but it is to be hoped that the surrounding herbage will soon spring high enough to hide it, or how will the fine purple eggs escape birds'-nesting schoolboys, not to mention hedge-hogs, stoats, and other four-footed enemies!

No such considerations seem to trouble the parents at present. With their nest completed, they flit about in the sun, calling frugally the while for "a little bit of bread and no cheese".

April

April

OF ALL THE ARTS and crafts of bird, beast, or man, the making of a chaffinch's nest seems to me to be the most delicately involved. Hair upon moss, wood upon hair, down upon wool, seems to be the formula; but the exact and traditional method of weaving and binding all these warm delicious softnesses none but the heir to all the ages of chaffinch experience and skill can possibly tell.

Apart from my profound admiration for his skill, the admiration of one whose own "fingers are all thumbs", I have a special fondness for this little bird, the "Pink", as they call him in some districts. He is so sturdy and cheerful, with his rose-coloured breast, and wing feathers picked out so smartly with white. Even in winter, when the other birds hang cold-puffed, like brown feathered fruit on the leafless boughs, he manages to hop and strut and pick a morsel here and there and appear thankful. But he is a bad neighbour. Let but half a dozen seeds escape the rake and he will spy them, gobble them up, and dig for more. He has cleared more than one bed of my sowing; but I bear him no malice. I should have covered them more neatly! . . .

The cuckoo is no favourite of mine. Judged by a human standard, its morals are altogether too questionable. In vain does my naturalist friend explain earnestly and at great length that, on account of some peculiarity in the formation of the breastbone, the hen cuckoo is physically incapable of sitting on her own eggs as other birds do, and, therefore, acts as a prudent mother in putting them out to nurse. Interesting as it all is to listen to, the heart does not warm to the cuckoo as it does to the tiny nest-makers, the Jenny-wren or the blue-tit.

So as it is not love for the bird itself which causes the thrill, it must be delight in the associations connected with its coming. It is not so much the cuckoo we welcome as cuckoo-time, the veritable sweet o' the year in this green and pleasant land of ours.

Or perhaps the new psychologists would trace it to the pleasurable emotion of childhood; for were we not taught then that upon hearing the first cuckoo call in the season every one of us was entitled to one wish, a fairy wish bound to come true? And, as we took care to wish audibly, and were not too ambitious, did the magic not invariably work?...

The hedgehog seems to be growing scarcer. At one time it was a common experience to meet with one in a country walk, but now often a whole season passes without sighting a prickle. Perhaps the gypsies thinned them when they camped so much upon the downs during the war. Many a one, I know, formed the chief ingredient in the stews which used to smell so deliciously when all the rest of the world went hungry. Formerly, not only the gypsies, but the poorer cottagers used to look upon the hedgehog as a very desirable addition to the *menu*. Those who have tasted the flesh say it resembles both chicken and pork. A very savoury combination!

The hedgehog has a bad character. In Sussex the country people firmly believe that in the short, light nights around midsummer, when the cows lie out all night in the pasture, the hedgehog creeps up to them and takes his toll from the overflowing udders. This may happen sometimes, for the hedgehog is extremely fond of milk when kept as a garden pet, but that the cows would permit a systematic milking by such prickly milkmaids is very doubtful.

The pool just now is as populous as a crowded city. Mallards and moorhens screech among the reed-beds; water rats "plop" in from the banks; fishes and other aquatic things make long ripples and splashes; the shallows are alive with tadpoles, darting and wriggling through the water in a kind of ordered dance.

How prodigal nature is of the frog-tribe! From the myriads of tadpoles one might foresee the whole valley full of them. Not one in a thousand, probably not one in ten thousand, will come to maturity, for the tadpole of the frog is beset with enemies; not a creature which lives in or near the water disdains to take a gulp of them, whole families at one mouthful, when no better game offers.

One day last week there were seven swans upon the pool. Returning migrants, perhaps, resting upon their way to more distant quarters. To-day there were three – number of ill-omen! The mated pair sailed regnant round and round the clear middle waters, necks arched, eyes supercilious, their snowiness mirrored. The odd one crouched, a dejected heap of white feathers, in a reed-bed by the margin.

It must have sustained some injury in a recent battle, for now and again it stretched a pinion and uttered one loud disconsolate "Squak!" One might have thought the noble pair above spite or petty revenge, but alas! every time they passed upon their serene and beauteous way, first one, then the other, turned aside to give a savage peck at the vanquished foe.

As I gathered up my basket and reached up to pick a few sprays of cherry-blossom for the vases, swift, dark wings skimmed the lake and dipped to the water, than away into the blue. The best thing in all the year has happened. *The swallows have come back!* . . .

To no part of England does spring come with more enchanting loveliness than to these secluded valleys beneath the southern hills. Form has given place to colour. The stern, bare outlines of winter are softened with the young green mist of breaking buds and unfolding leaves. The heath and the hill, so dark and shaggy until a week ago, have burst into a conflagration of blossoming gorse; the water-meadows are gilded with dandelion and kingcup, and the garden fruit trees stand snowy against the April blue of the sky. Blue, green and gold are the predominating colours of earth, all melting and toning to a general brightness in the haze the sun draws from the still moist soil.

In the woods it is primrose time, and primrose time upon the Hampshire and Sussex borders is a pale yellow floodtide. Every copse is a primrose copse, and every lane a primrose path.

The scent of the primrose is the very breath of April. It is less a perfume than a fragrance, a sweet, fresh, wholesome scent, instinct with honesty and goodness, yet at the same time full of delicate suggestions.

It is strange how closely the sense of smell is associated with the memory. A whiff from a passing haycart in a city street; the scent of a flower in the hand of a passer-by; the leather of old book-bindings – even such odours as those of bread from the oven, mackintosh, homespun tweed, or cigar smoke may be potent to unlock the memory and transport the mind a hundred miles or a score of years.

For me the scent or sight of a primrose holds this magic. I never see, smell, or think of them but I am carried back at once to a day in the last April before the war. It was a day of warm sun and sunshine showers, and I stood alone upon one of the low wooded hills of the Isle of Wight.* All around and as far as I could see were primroses – primroses springing from the turf at my feet, breaking into foam at the edge of the clearing, and yellowing the land right down to the little grassy fields which fringed the cliffs.

A light shower had just fallen, and the scent of the flowers was indescribably fresh and sweet. As the sun reappeared a cuckoo began to call from a tree close by, and, as I straightened my back from my flower-picking to listen, I saw a rainbow spanning the steeples of Ryde in a perfect arch.

It was one of those rare moments which live in the memory for ever. Upon such occasions time halts for an instant, and the beauty of earth seems to quiver like a curtain veiling a hidden mystery. The startled beholder waits for a revelation. Alas! in the very moment of recognition the vision dissolves. But sometimes for our comfort a scent or a sound is consecrated in that moment and left with us as a charm to unlock that fugitive impression and make it live again.

One other flower shares the wet April woods beneath Peverel. The wood anemone is now in its fragile prime, swaying and bending with every breath of

---

*Flora Thompson was then living in Bournemouth.

air, and making the primrose by contrast appear sturdy. To-day in the very depths of the wood I came upon a pale wave of them. Just at that place the trees are so thickly planted that scarcely a sunbeam can penetrate, and a little later in the year the earth will be a tangle of fern and long grass. Even now, with only a sprinkling of green on the boughs, the shade is too deep for other flowers. A few primroses, pale and weak-stemmed, cluster about the pathway, but farther in the thicket are anemones only.

The Greeks called the wood anemone the wind-flower, and had many beautiful legends concerning it. One was that a nymph of Flora's Court attracted by her loveliness the attentions of Zephyr, whereupon the jealous goddess banished her to the gloom of the deepest woods. She pined so in her exile that Zephyr, seeking and finding her there, transformed her into the flower we still know by her name; and that is why she has ever since responded to his slightest caress.

Our own forefathers were of a more utilitarian turn of mind. They used the anemone as a charm against all bodily ills. Every year the first flower to be seen in bloom was plucked with the solemn invocation: "I gather thee as a charm against sickness." It was then carried home in the finder's bosom, wrapped ceremoniously in red cloth, and treasured in some secret spot until illness occurred. When that happened, it was bound upon the afflicted part of the patient, and in that position, no doubt, was as efficacious as many modern remedies; for, if it did no good, at least it did no harm, and formed a peg to hang faith on . . .

The birds most in evidence about Peverel now are the lapwings. They have come back in great numbers, and nest so close together, ten or twelve couples within a hundred yards, that they always appear to be in a flock.

It is a beautiful sight to see the handsome, glossy, black and white birds, with crested heads proudly erect, run swiftly over the daisied grass, or flap overhead against the blue sky, uttering their plaintive and melancholy "Pee-wit!" In a week or two the hen, when she runs, will be followed by her brood, for, like most of the earth-nesting birds, the lapwing can run as soon as it leaves the shell. When that time comes there will be a sinister shadow upon the sunny sward – a shadow with the motion of wings – for the kestrel will be abroad.

There is so much this month to be seen and done that the days, lengthening as they are, are not half long enough. A garden alone is one person's work, or would be if it were properly attended to, which mine is not. Instead, I clear little islands in the green, and plant out in them whatever comes handy. It is not proper gardening, I know, but in practice it works out fairly well, for

between the beds and along the pathways I have planted quantities of all the large old-fashioned perennials, larkspur, delphinium, southernwood, and lavender, and they have grown and spread until they conceal a whole wilderness of bad management. There are ferns, too, a great number of them, for this is a fern country; but they, at present, are but brown scaley curled-up balls with, here and there, the tiniest, shyest feather of green peeping.

This spring, on the whole, the garden does not quite come up to the standard of my dreams when I planned it. It is "they dratted birds," as the old man who sometimes comes to dig for me is so fond of saying. The sparrows pluck out the tender shoots and the chaffinches disinter most of the seeds I plant; but, if all he says is true, and I cannot have both birds and blossoms, I will be content with none, or very few of the latter, for, after all, the whole valley is just one garden now, and to all intents and purposes mine, for nobody else comes near it.

Down by the pool the grass grows lush and long again after its winter soaking; the trees, though still leafless, are reddish-purple with rising sap and quickening buds; the banks are gay with celandine, wild forget-me-not, and the meek-eyed innocence of Star of Bethlehem. There are violets, too, for those who know where to look for them, white violets, mostly, and a peculiar pinkish-purple shade I have never seen elsewhere. But best of all are the daffodils.

These latter are my especial pride and delight. I watched the first green spears shoot up in February, knew when the first bud appeared, was sorry when the rain beat them down to earth, and glad when the sun coaxed them upright. Now they are out in full beauty, a long yellow pool, like sunshine spilt beneath the trees on the farther shore of the lake. I could gather whole sheaves of them if I wished without leaving the slightest gap; but I do not, for they look so perfect where they are that it seems a shame to bring them indoors to be parched by the fire and lamplight.

The memory of my discovery of these wild daffodils is amongst my earliest impressions of life upon Peverel. That, the scent of wood fires, the clean, cold feeling of newly distempered walls; and, yes, one thing more, the constant re-echoing of a line I had come across in my reading:

"The kiss of God is cold."

I do not know whence it is taken. I think it must have been quoted, or I should surely remember the rest; but for a time that one line pervaded my consciousness, repeating itself over and over until it became a kind of sacred charm to me. . .

Of all country sights the most distressing is the taking of a small bird by a hawk. Passing a ploughed field last winter I was suddenly aware of a commotion amongst a flock of chaffinches pecking amongst the clods. The shrill shrieks of the birds were so expressive of terror that I stopped to investigate. At that moment a hawk rose from the midst of them with a victim in its claws. The cries of the bird as it was carried through the air were piteous in the extreme; gradually they grew weaker and weaker, but whether death or distance silenced them I could not tell.

To a human onlooker such a sight is most painful. Nothing can be done, for the hawk scarcely touches the earth, but swoops, seizes its prey, and soars again, to descend and enjoy its meal in some unknown and far distant spot. The strange part of the tragedy in this case was the behaviour of the other birds. Though terrified enough while the hawk was amongst them, as soon as it had soared aloft they resumed their pecking, and were chirping happily again before the dying cries of their small comrade had ceased.

Those cries of terror rang in my ears for days, and the sight of a hawk hovering above the heath filled me with loathing. Yet the kestrel only acted according to its nature. The victim suffered, it is true, but the hawk, for the sake of its own convenience, would be certain to despatch it as expeditiously as it could; and hawks have to get a living as well as chaffinches. And then, are *we* quite sure that sheep and oxen suffer no terror in slaughter-houses? If we are not, we have no reason to consider ourselves superior in that respect to the kestrel, and all our tenderness verges upon sentimentality . . .

Every year upon Peverel at about this time the three or four bats which have haunted the heath upon mild nights since the frost broke up are increased to a score or more.

Where they come from is a mystery, for there is no old barn or church tower at all near, but there they are, swooping and tumbling against the darkening sky, only their queer, flittering wing movement and shrill mousey squeak distinguishing them from the graceful birds they contrive to caricature in the half-light.

As soon as the swallows arrive the bats will decrease in numbers; so perhaps it is a case of supply and demand – the insects are hatched out by the sun, and the bats suddenly spring from nowhere to enjoy a supper of them; then the swallows come, assert their superior right, and the bats retire.

No animal is more social in its hibernating habits than the bat. Not only do they sleep in companies, but they actually cling together in their sleep. The sexton of an old Sussex church once told me that a few years ago, when his tower was under repair, a large and interlocked mass of the sleeping creatures was discovered by a workman beneath the leads. They were hanging by their claws, heads downward, and the man detached them and sent them down in the wooden cage used to haul his tools up and down. And there, as my friend related, they lay upon a grave in the sun, "for all the world like a girt bundle o' rusty old leather".

The workmen wanted to destroy them, but the sexton objected, for what, as he said, is a belfry without a few bats about it? So, one by one they came to life in the warmth, and flapped off around the tower and away, looking, as he repeated, "most darn'd unnater'l in the daylight!" . . .

April is the sweetest of all the months according to our poets, for what other season has been sung in English as April has? So greatly has April been loved, indeed, that it is one of the few months that have been personified. Shakespeare, when he wrote of "proud-pied April, dressed in all his trim," saw it as a youth, or perhaps a boy, full of the pride of life, changeable with ever varying desires and bright with conquering beauty. Other poets have visualised April as a maiden, full of the feminine traits of changeableness and charm. Sir William Watson painted her portrait well for us when he sang -

> "April, April,
> Laugh, thy girlish laughter,
> Then, the moment after,
> Weep thy girlish tears."

It is this feminine quality of constant change which is April's greatest charm. There is no blue like the blue of skies smiling from recent showers; no sunshine quite so bright as that reflected by the wet earth, and the songs the birds sing with their wings still wet sound more joyous than any other songs.

In freshness and delicacy of tint, too, April is altogether virginal. Green and white of daisied turf, of burgeoning hedgerows and blossoming orchards; blue and white of cloud-piled skies and silver slant of sunshine showers; these are April's own colours. The deeper tints of tulips and forget-me-nots in the garden beds, of flowering currant in the shrubbery, and the deep crimson of forest buds against the sky are rather the embroidery upon the hem of her garment than the pattern of it.

The chief wild-flowers of the month are light in colour. The primrose is delicately pale, the daisy faintly blushing, the blackthorn purely snowy. The violet alone glows with decided colour, and that is a scent rather than a colour-note, for it hides its sweetness in its wet leaves and makes no show in the landscape.

This general delicacy of tint holds no monotony. The greens of the foliage of the different trees alone make endless variety. Amongst the opening leaves may be found every gradation of the tint, from the strong, standard green of the hawthorn hedge to the silvery white beam on one hand, and the purplish-green of the copper-beech on the other . . .

The swallow birds, especially the house-martins, have a great deal of hard work before them before the first long spell of dry weather sets in. Ideal April weather affords them exactly the proper conditions they need for their nest-building, and that, no doubt, is the reason they set to work mending their old nests and setting the foundations of new ones the very moment they arrive. To suit them, the weather must be neither too wet nor too dry. Rain, of course, they must have, or where would the mud for their masonry come from? But rain in moderation, with intervals of sun and wind, or the mud would not only be too liquid to work, but too soft to set and harden as it should.

The building of a swallow's nest is a skilled and arduous process. Thousands of mud pellets must be collected and carried greater or less distances, and these must not be daubed together at random as they are collected, but set in a certain immemorial manner, and each course which goes to form the little mud-cup cradles we see beneath our eaves must be allowed to dry and set before the next is added to it . . .

The colouring of a bird's egg is usually the first feature to strike an observer, for not only is it a great beauty of many eggs, but it is also the most obvious clue as to what bird it belongs. Many of our common hedgerow birds lay beautifully tinted eggs, and one of April's wonders is the coarse little brown nest of the hedge sparrow, with its four or five turquoise treasures arranged point to point in the centre, each egg shell as soft as satin and as warm as brooding love can keep it.

Several other hedgerow birds' eggs also show different shades of blue, from the clear sky-colour of the thrush, to the dim mottled bluish-grey of the blackbird. Others, again, are white, mottled or flecked with red, such as those of the robin and most of the warbler families. In the eggs of the yellowhammer this reddish shade is deepened to almost a purple, while the red-flecked ground of the linnet's egg is bluish-grey.

All the above, and many other coloured eggs belong to birds which build in safe positions above ground level. Those which make the bare earth their nursery cannot afford to indulge in brightly-coloured eggs, as they would be too conspicuous. So the ground-nesting birds, with very few exceptions, lay eggs more or less of an earth-tint. The skylark, for instance, lays her dark grey and brown mottled clutch almost openly upon the bare earth, merely choosing some slight depression nearer a taller tuft of grass than ordinary; yet, so perfect is the protective colouring of her eggs that, as many of my readers know, a lark's nest, even when once found, can seldom be come upon a second time.

The outstanding exceptions to this rule of "an earth-nesting bird, an earth-coloured egg", are those of the game birds, partridge and pheasant. Both of these lay eggs of a warm cream-colour, but, as in both cases the number in a clutch exceeds a dozen, a wide margin is left for casualties, and this probably is designed to serve the same end as protective colouring does in the four or five-egg clutches of the other ground-laying birds.

Pure white eggs placed against green or brown would be the most conspicuous of all if easily accessible, so we usually find the bird which lays a white egg hides its nest more carefully than other kinds. The owl, deep in its hollow tree trunk, or high up in the seclusion of an ivied tower, can afford to lay an egg so white that, even in the gloomy half-darkness, it strikes the eye immediately. The wood-pigeon lays its two white eggs in the tree tops, and the kingfisher her six or eight in a dark burrow in the river bank.

Smaller white egg-laying birds hide their clutch away in the recesses of elaborately-constructed nests. The wren does so, and the willow-warbler,

while the long-tailed tit weaves a bottle-shaped nest with a lid to it. Whether these nesting habits were first adopted to hide dangerously conspicuous eggs, or whether long ages of concealed nesting has done away with pro-tective colouring in certain cases, is a question we may leave to the scientists. Perhaps, originally, all eggs were white, and colour was evolved to suit circum-stances – the blue egg to tone with the sky as the eye of the searcher looked up through the boughs, and the green, grey and brown to harmonise with the grass and soil and stones. As to this, we can only speculate; but, whether the wonder was worked directly by creation, or gradually by evolution, the marvel is no less.

The size of the different eggs, varying with every kind of bird, and not always in proportion to its size, is also most probably governed by circum-stances. As a general rule, the eggs of the ground-nesting birds are larger according to their sizes than those which build in a safer position, for a large egg means a good supply of nourishment for the embryo chick, ensuring that it shall not be hatched out until it is large and strong enough almost immediately to take care of itself; while a tiny egg signifies a bald, blind, and helpless baby bird, which will need the protection of its parents and the shelter of a snug nest for at least a fortnight.

So we see emerge from the egg in the open nest upon the ground a young bird, well-covered with down and able to run and hide from enemies within a few hours of its birth; while from the small egg in the cosy nest will come a blind, weak and naked atom, which will only become fledged by degrees, and will even require food, warmth and, later on, flying lessons from its devoted parents.

Eggs in the nest, if touched at all by human hand, should be dealt with most tenderly, for there is nothing a mother bird objects to more than interference, and, if her clutch is much handled, or her arrangement of the eggs disturbed, she is likely to desert the nest altogether. The best way to examine a nest is to wait until both parents are absent upon a food foraging expedition, then to contrive to get into a position in which it is possible to look down upon without touching the eggs. If the natural desire to touch them is too strong to be resisted, they may be lightly stroked with the finger tips without lifting them or altering the arrangement.

Thus gently to touch the egg of a song-bird, so smooth and warm and dry, while keen spring winds shake the boughs above and the leaves maybe are dripping from recent showers, is one of the most delicately thrilling experi-ences the nature-lover receives from the earth about him . . .

Just within the wood, a large patch of dog's mercury makes mimic sunshine even when the sky is overcast. Clustered in circles round the axils of the half-unfurled leaves, the long, thin flowerspikes are really more green than yellow, but the whole effect of so many in a mass is sunny.

It is interesting to note the manner in which the leaf bud of this humble plant is protected, the young stems being bent forward at the tip, and each individual leaf so rolled that the strong, rough midrib is uppermost, so that the naturally weak and tender shoots may have strength to pierce the thick mat of moss and dead leaves always to be found in the shady places it favours . . .

Soon the tiny nest of the whitethroat will be found by those who do not mind wading through briars and nettles to where it is placed a few inches above ground-level in the heart of a scrubby thicket. Even before the greenish-white, red-mottled eggs appear, it may be distinguished by the cotton-woolly willow-catkins the birds love to weave with the coarse bents and horse-hair of the foundation.

The lesser whitethroat is smaller than the above-mentioned bird, but resembles it closely in colouring. Gilbert White, the father of British bird-study, whose country parish of Selborne joins the one in which these notes are written, has left us a fascinating description of the lesser whitethroat.

"This bird," he says, "has a white, or rather silvery, breast and body; is restless and active, like the willow wren, and hops from bough to bough, examining every part for food. It also runs up the stems of the crown-imperials, and, putting its head into the bells of these flowers, sips the liquor which stands in the nectarium of each petal."*

A charming picture, but one I have never had the good fortune to see, for, as far as I have observed, the whitethroat does not sip from any other flower, and the crown-imperial for some reason or other has long since disappeared from this locality.

I wonder if many of my readers know it? A kind of lily, sometimes brown, sometimes yellow, but with blooms more bell-shaped than those of most lilies, growing in a ring round a tuft of bright green leaves at the top of a tall, rod-like stem. When one of the bells is lifted, a ring of mother-o'-pearl discs may be seen at the bottom of the cup, one at the base of each petal; and it was one of the puzzles of my childhood whether the flower took its name from these interior pearls – the local version being "crown o' pearls" – or from the crown of bell-shaped blossoms at the top of the stem.

In those days a tuft of crown-imperial was always used to crown the garland which was carried from door to door on May Day. A garland, not like the mop of flowers still carried on a stick in some country places, but a solid structure of

---

*The Natural History of Selborne, Letter LVII.

interlaced hoops of flowers, about the same size and shape as the crinolines we see in pictures of early Victorian times. This garland, with its crowning plume of crown-imperials, not only taxed the resources of every garden in the place, but also the strength of the two tallest girls in the village school, who bore it between them on a long white staff.

Only once have I seen the cherished plant in recent years; then it was from the top of a 'bus which had halted in a suburban road. It was a street of poor cottages, only a shade above squalor; the tiny front gardens were mostly given over to the dusty earthworks of the children, but one garden bed of the whole long line was well kept, and in that stood a few rods of the imperial flower.

It was good to see it again, though most of its charm was lost in its incongruous surroundings; for the present faded, and the mind went back to the cottage garden, full of wallflower, forget-me-not and polyanthus, where the crown-imperials were the choicest treasure of the sun-bonneted old dame who spent most of her waking hours watching her beehives and guarding the flowers she grew for the benefit of her bees from the snatching little fingers that *would* creep through the white palings.*

Once a year she opened her heart – and her garden – to the children, filled their hands with the more abundant spring flowers, and to the eldest girl, properly accredited from the schoolmistress, sacrificed at least half of her crown-imperial spikes. That, as far as I can remember, was the only time she spoke to anyone, the rest of the year was devoted to her beehives.

These stood in a long line beneath a hedge of flowering currant, not painted wooden houses, such as hive the pampered insects of to-day, but yellow straw skips, each roofed by a red pan, weighted down by a stone. On a three-legged stool beside them their mistress would sit dreaming and dozing for a whole summer day together, a little old woman in a mauve sun-bonnet and plaid shawl who might have dropped straight out of a fairy-tale.

Now and again, in early summer, a loud hubbub would arise in the sleepy garden – a sound of beating and drumming, tinkling and jangling; and then the villagers would smile at each other and say: "Old Sally's bees've a'swarmed"; and anyone near enough would see the old woman rushing wildly backwards and forwards, bonnet strings flying, as she followed the flight of a column of whirling wings, banging all the time with her door key upon whatever pot or pan had come nearest.

---

*This passage contains strong echoes of the opening of chapter V of *Lark Rise,* although the practice of tanging the bees is there ascribed not to Sally but to Queenie.

One day I ventured to ask her why she did this. Her answer was emphatic, if confused. First of all she said the "tanging", as she called it, pacified the bees and induced them to settle immediately. Pressed farther, she declared it was "the law"; that if she failed to tang her own bees with her own front door-key when they swarmed, and to keep up the tanging until they settled, she lost all claim upon them if they happened to stray beyond her garden bounds.

Very likely she was right, that, if it was no longer the law, it had once been so, and she was the last to remember or observe it, for her bright blue eyes spoke of Saxon origin, and, when she referred to houses, she said "housen". At any rate, listening to her then, it seemed to youth that she might have been there, watching her bees, from the time when a King who was also a Saint was on the throne.

Survival or not, she did not tang her bees much longer. At my next visit to the place, after an interval of years, cottage, garden, beehives and mistress were gone like a dream. Only the yew tree she had clipped into the semblance of a rooster remained, and that, frayed and distorted, stood in the corner of a ploughed field.

Cottage, garden and busy beehives had all vanished with their mistress, and yet it seemed upon that bright spring morning that the furrowed field was not quite common earth, or whence came the rich perfume of wallflower and primrose? And what caused the bees to collect about the few poor flowering weeds in quite such a murmurous multitude?

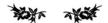

May

May

*T*HE BLUEBELL, or wild hyacinth as they call it in Scotland, is my best beloved of all spring flowers; for me, as soon as it appears, the primrose, and even the violet, turns pale beside its rich and darkly glowing beauty.

In olden times, they say, the bluebell of England played almost as important a part in human sentiment as the bluebell of Scotland does now. The Greeks wore it as a token of remembrance, and engraved it as such upon the tombs of their loved ones. In England, before the heyday of the rose, it was known as "the flower of St. George". Blooming, as it does, about his day, it was used, no doubt, to fashion garlands in his honour. Young girls wore it wreathed in their hair at the weddings of their friends. Modern bridesmaids might go to the farthest florist and fare no better!

But, although we no longer express our fancies so poetically, it is still a general favourite. Stand on any Sunday evening in May at any tram terminus upon the outskirts of a city, watch the returning crowds, and you will see that two out of three of the women and children carry bluebells. Sometimes it makes one a little sad to see, for often they have been pulled instead of plucked, and the long blanched lower stems are a sorry sight; sometimes, too, they are cast aside to be churned to an unpleasant-looking pulp in the dust. But I like to think that for every single abandoned stalk fifty fresh and living ones are brightening some poor room with beauty. . .

The bluebell is so overwhelming in its loveliness, and so much a feature of the woods at this season, that at a casual glance one might conclude it was the only flower in bloom. That would be a great mistake; at least a score of other seasonable plants are in flower, not to mention the lingerers, languid primroses upon pale, threadlike stems, and the last violets, so engulfed in leaves that only the scent betrays them.

Most delicate and tender amongst the newcomers, the wood-sorrel droops its white, purple-veined little cup above a bank of vivid trefoil leaves. These leaves of the wood-sorrel are even more beautiful than the delicate, fragile flower is; for they shade through every tint of green, and, with their sharp, clear outline and veining, have a finished, jewel-like appearance. But, in reality, nothing could be farther from the glitter and hardness of gems; the wood-sorrel, leaf and flower, is a very miracle of fragility. Pluck a leaf, and it wilts visibly; to carry a nosegay of the flowers even for a yard or two is an impossibility, and that, perhaps, is why it is less known than almost any other flower of spring.

Yet, little as it is regarded now, it must once have been a great favourite, for its names are many, a different one for almost every county. In some parts it is called "Cuckoo's Bread", in others "Gowk's Meat", while yet others maintain it to be the true and original shamrock.

But the most beautiful name of all, and one, so far as I know, fallen to complete disuse now, is that attributed to it by the old writer Gerarde: "The apothecaries and herbalists," he says, "call it alleluya, because it springeth forth and flourisheth at the time when alleluya is wont to be sung in churches." The old name is lost, but the erstwhile bearer of it lives on and still "praises God with sweetest looks" at this most joyful time of the year.

When the sun disappears behind a cloud, and rain or cold air chills the woodlands, the little wood-sorrel closes both flower and leaf, just as it does at night. Even on bright days, if the wind is cold or the hot sun strikes too directly upon it, it furls itself, for it is a thing of the shade and cool green recesses, a delicate, fastidious thing, created to satisfy another mood in man from that in which he glories in the tulip and the rose . . .

The wood, for all its gay freshness, has its tragedies. Of the pheasant's nest I mentioned last month only a scooped-out hollow filled with fragments of broken egg-shells remains. Through the debris a long green finger of bracken has sprung up to emphasise the deserted coldness.

What form the catastrophe took which befell the nest and eggs is uncertain. Something silent-footed and bright-eyed, there is no doubt. Perhaps the nest was raided by a stoat or weasel, or even one of the pretty, innocent-seeming squirrels which abound there; for all of these creatures are fond of eggs, and would not hesitate to make such a dainty meal if they called and found the hen-bird "not at home".

The pair of blackbirds in the bush above it have been more fortunate. Their brood is out, and the fledglings were taking their first flying lesson this morning. It was amusing to see them, so heavy and helpless, fluttering a few yards, then sinking to earth, or hiding sulkily under leaves and grasses and pretending not to hear the encouraging "chirrups" of their patient mother. By the end of the week they will be up and away to fend for themselves, and the parent birds will begin preparing for a second brood.

The blackbirds have almost accomplished the task of bringing up one family; other birds have their responsibilities before them. The sand-martins, lately back from over-seas, are extremely busy furbishing up their old nests in the face of the sandstone cliff of the disused sand-pit upon the heath.

It is pleasant to watch them swooping down from the blue and hanging by their tiny claws to the threshold of the holes in which their homes are. The soft-tawney-golden rock is riddled all about the upper part by these small openings, like little windows, for it is an old colony, and the birds return to it year after year.

The sand-martin is smaller and not so handsome of plumage as its cousins, the swallow and house-martin. The metallic lustre of the latter birds is toned down in the sand-martin to gentle greys and browns, but its shape is much the same as theirs, and its flight as graceful and sweeping, so that there is no danger of mistaking the family to which it belongs. Usually it returns to England about the end of April, but those in this locality were, for some reason or other, rather later than usual this year, and the cleaning and renovating of their nests is still in full swing.

The tunnelling of the rock in the first place is an extraordinary feat for so small and seemingly weak a creature. The young birds in search of a new settlement select some cliff, river bank, or railway cutting, and, hanging on to the perpendicular surface with their claws, excavate with their bills. If they come to a stone or other unyielding substance, they peck round and round until they loosen it; if it proves too large for negotiation, the place is abandoned, and they begin all over again in another spot.

Some of these small caverns are said to go back to a depth of two feet or more; others are shallow cavities, just deep enough to shelter the nest. Much, no doubt, depends upon the aspect and nature of the soil.

The house-martins have completed their abode beneath the eaves of the cottage. I hear their last goodnight twitter as I write. In the wide space of twilight sky before the window another creature which might in this light be mistaken for a relative of theirs is on the wing.

But the sweeping and swooping flier is not a swallow, not a bird of any kind; it is a furred, and not a feathered, thing, which is hawking for insects above the dark outline of the downs. The bat, like the sand-martin, has only just reappeared. All the winter it has slept, head downward, hanging by the claws from some rafter in barn or belfry. Now it is back in the night sky, uttering its sharp little squeak, and pleasing as much by its quaintness as other things do by their beauty . . .

The lane where I picked my speedwell and stitchwort this morning is at present a flower-garden. It is an old and almost disused cart-track, leading from the main road to the open heights of Peverel. Once it was broad and open, for in the old days it was a coaching road running into the main road from London to the sea. Now it is grassed over and half-choked with boughs. A few cottages dotted about the heath close by keep it open; the baker's van and the coal-cart come that way once or twice a week; children go to school by it, and women to their shopping, but it is quite possible to spend a whole morning there without seeing anyone.

By the sides of the footpath and between the cart-ruts, rabbits nibble the turf to a velvety pile; but in the shadow of the hedge the grass is long and mossy, and splashed about with mauve pools of dog-violet and ground-ivy. The overhanging hedgerows are composed of gnarled old bushes – hawthorn and witch-hazel, and the rarer spindle-berry. This thick greenery is a sanctuary for birds. Within the space of a dozen yards yellowhammers, blue-tits, robins, wrens, and blackbirds have their lodgings. Flitting from bush to bush to-day was a bevy of long-tailed tits, eight of them, quaint tiny things, in rose and grey. They would settle upon a spray of hawthorn, each small head upon one side in a listening attitude, each tail, longer than the rest of its owner's body, quivering upward; then, reassured of their safety, peck and peck again, each at its appointed knot of bloom, until the supply of whatever insect or caterpillar they were feasting upon was exhausted.

One bird seemed to be leader of the expedition. He would utter a sudden small "Cheep!" and fly off to a fresh bush, followed by the other seven in single file. I do not know if they were an early brood, bred in the lane. They may have been, for the ivy and lichens of the aged bushes must contain just such cosy nooks as they love to nest in. Or they may have been a party of adults taking an outing in company, for the long-tailed tit has a sociable nature and loves to fly in bands, even in the nesting season.

Floating over them as they pecked at their hawthorn buds, the crab-apple by the gateway cast a shower of petals, like rosy-tinted snow. Little gusts of wind caught them and sent them in drifts down the lane, until the grass was sprinkled and the air filled with their clean, delicate fragrance. That they, with their subtle scent and delicate texture, should be born of such a tree seemed miraculous; for never was crab-apple so dark and tough, so tortured by winds and broken by raids upon the deceptive red and yellow of its fruit as that one.

It is a tree with a story. Long years ago, they say, a poor man hung himself upon a branch of it. In the cold grey of dawn, as his workmates passed, they saw him in the gateway, swaying to and fro, as they thought in pain. Only when they came quite near could they see that his feet were an inch or two off the earth. Poor sufferer! A series of calamities had unhinged his mind. May he rest in peace. Somehow, that even the branch he bore down with his weight should break into blossom again speaks of hope for him . . .

The introduction of the egg of the cuckoo into the nest of its selected foster-parents is one of the wonders of bird life. The hen cuckoo does not lay the egg straight into the nest. That would be too long a proceeding: the real mistress of the dwelling might return, when there would certainly be a scene. No. The cuckoo has far more tact. She lays her egg at leisure upon the ground, then, taking it in her bill, flies swiftly and deposits it in some nest previously selected. Generally the nests selected are those of the hedge-sparrow, chaffinch, or one of the warblers; for the cuckoo lays an egg remarkably small

for a bird of her size, and if the eggs already in the nest were much larger or smaller the trick would be discovered at once.

As it is, when the unsuspecting foster-mother returns she notices nothing unusual, or, if she does, is deluded into thinking she had lost count of her rapidly growing family. When the eggs are hatched the young cuckoo passes for some time as a hedge-sparrow, chaffinch, or wagtail, as the case may be. One bird among the brood, it is true, has an inordinate appetite, cries continually for food, and gulps it ravenously; but the mother's labour is well repaid by seeing the rate at which that one amongst her nestlings flourishes. By the end of a fortnight it is much larger and stronger than its foster-brethren, and so it goes on; for not only does it consume double rations, robbing others of their just dues, but it is destined to be a much larger bird in later life, and has much headway to make up.

Presently the tragedy occurs. The young cuckoo has taken to the middle of the nest, to burrowing down in the soft woolly bottom and, with a flicking movement of its wings, tossing the other nestlings upward until they rest upon its own back. One by one they go over the edge, and their half-fledged corpses dangle upon boughs or rot in the grasses below, while the deluded mother continues to slave for the usurper. To our human ideas this is a cruel and unnatural arrangement on the part of Nature. But hedge-sparrows are plentiful and cuckoos scarce!. . .

No age can have everything, and in material ways ours is more fortunate than any preceding one. We have our wireless, a daily fireside miracle; our quick transport, which would have seemed almost as miraculous to our ancestors; the blessings of modern surgery and medicine to prolong life; machinery to shorten our labour, and merchandise brought from the ends of the earth to make us comfortable.

With these and all our other advantages in hand, it seems ungracious to look back with any touch of envy to the past; yet there are times when we feel that modern comfort has been too dearly bought, and that we would gladly exchange our twentieth-century conveniences for a share of that innocent joy of life which our ancestors accepted as a matter of course. Not that the men and women of Merrie England escaped sorrow and suffering; they had, indeed, more than their full human share of them; but an easy conscience, largely due to the unshaken faith of the time, left each one of them a margin of spiritual energy with which to enjoy life.

It is better to take a hard life lightly than an easy life hardly, and our ancestors appear to have mastered the art of living better than we are able to do. The housewife took a pride in her house, the husbandman in his fields, the artisan in his craft; but for them these important matters were not the whole of life. When work was done, they were just as ready to throw themselves into play as they had been into work, and play for them did not mean a feverish expenditure of money and energy, but a placid enjoyment of the homely pleasures at their doors. Foremost amongst these were the pleasures brought by the changing seasons – the harvest-home supper, the Christmas mummings, or the celebration of the feast-day of the saint to whom the village church was dedicated.

Gayest and most lighthearted of all were the May-day revels.* After the long closed-in winter, the first of May came as the most important and long-looked-forward-to landmark in the year. Then they might, as their proverbs said, "throw candle and candlestick right away", "cast" as many "clouts" as they felt inclined to, and go forth into a world freshly decorated for the feast to take their natural part in the general rejoicing.

On every village green a maypole was raised and crowned with garlands; the May Queen was chosen; there were games for the children, dancing on the green for the young, and good home-brewed, flavoured with pleasant chat, for the elders.

This day of all the year was the People's Day – not only of those classes which now appropriate the term, but of the People as a whole. None were too rich and proud or too poor and humble to participate in a pleasure which need cost nothing and was open to all. The Lady of the Manor, in her stiff brocade, moved freely amongst the grey and scarlet clad village-wives. Her daughters,

*See *Lark Rise*, chapter XIII.

like theirs, had been up and out at dawn to wash their faces in the morning dew, and now tripped as gaily upon the greensward, setting to partners with the young yeomen with as much zest as they would to "m'Lord" in the London ballrooms on their rare visits to town.

Nor was the feast exclusively a country merrymaking. Town Squares and Market Places had their maypoles too. London itself raised one yearly in the Strand, and one of the noblest of our queens-consort went maying to Greenwich Hill to dip her face in the dew.

In later years, after the maypole had become a thing of the past, the children still kept up the festival, ranging the flower-decked and dew-besprinkled countryside on May morning, showing their garlands at every house, and waking late sleepers with a shrill

> "A bunch of May I have brought you,
> And at your door it stands;
> It is but a sprout, but it's well put about
> By the Lord Almighty's hands."

Later still, within the memory of many of us, this garland carrying degenerated into a mere begging for pennies, and then, indeed, the glory had departed from the May.

Other times, other manners. No more shall we see a maypole in the Strand, or hear of a Queen of England dipping her face in May-dew. The May festivities have been revived in a few places, it is true, and the motorist on a country road may sometimes come across a maypole with streamers and garlands complete; but these new May revels are as far as possible removed in spirit from those of the past. Those were the expression of a spontaneous and general rejoicing: these are more of a nature of an entertainment organized by a few superior persons for the good of a not too willing public. Although kindly planned, such revivals fall rather flat; the new maypole is an alien and exotic thing to a populace with a taste for American films and the fox-trot. The well-drilled school-children who dance around it are somewhat too conscientious for joy; the spectators of the humbler sort have to be bribed with tea and buns to attend. The spirit of oneness with Nature and joy in her rebirth which inspired the May rejoicings in the past has taken other forms to-day.

That that spirit remains inherent in man is shown by many signs. The holiday rush from town to country, the increasing number of periodicals devoted to nature study, the advertisement of "beauty spots" by railway and motor-coach companies – all go to show that some contact with earth, however second hand or muffled, is still a prime necessity of humankind. And, if this new nature-cult lacks organized expression, we may still feel that a bond of sympathy unites nature-lovers all over the country, and that our joy in this loveliest of months is shared by a fraternity of invisible friends . . .

For man, with his thirst for knowledge as well as beauty, the mechanism of the bluebell holds endless wonders. At first the flower-stalk stands erect with its unopened buds; then, as the lower bells unclose, the stem droops over and takes the graceful curve which is part of its loveliness. Then, when the flowers are over, the stem rises erect again, and holds the fat green seed-cases up to be ripened by the sun.

The leaves are still more wonderfully arranged. The bluebell is one of our so-called self-irrigating plants, and every leaf is furnished with a number of little gutters by which the rain is conducted to the roots. If a leaf is bent very gently backwards and forwards in such a manner as to partly separate it, it will be found to contain a number of minute white threads which can be stretched like elastic. These threads are supposed to be furnished to strengthen the soft, fleshy leaf against the wind, and each thread is not, as it appears at first, one straight filament, but composed of a spiral coil, similar to the watch-spring steels used by corset-makers.

The whole of the plant – root, leaf, and flower-stalk – is full of a sticky, milk-like fluid which, although highly poisonous, was once useful to man in a number of ways. The archer of the Middle Ages used it as a gum to affix his arrow-heads; the monk for his bookbinding; the lady of Elizabethan times to stiffen the high neck-ruffs which figure so prominently in the portraits of her day . . .

All the perfumes of May are delicious. The lilac sets the predominating scent in the garden, fresh and pure and hauntingly sweet; then upon the hills there is the rich, warm, ripe-fruit and almond flavour of the gorse, while away in the valleys whole regions are filled with the rainy freshness of the hawthorn. But the scent of the woods is more subtle than these; it is compounded of a thousand fragrances: the hyacinth perfume of the bluebell is in it, the spiciness of pine, and the moist freshness of moss and fern and tree-bark.

Our great-grandmothers, who did not depend upon laboratories for their perfumes as we do, but distilled them for themselves, cherishing each receipt as a family secret, had one great favourite for filling the little gold filigree pomanders they carried at their waists, which they called "Scent o'th' May". The secret of its making has perished with the fashion for it, but the very name breathes to the imagination from the printed page, tempting each one of us to reconstruct it in fancy. There would certainly be lilac in it, and a few hawthorn petals, if only for the sake of the name; then wallflower, and the tender young buds of sweetbriar, and apple-blossom, too, if, even with their still-room skill, they were able to capture a sweetness so subtle . . .

Where, a week ago, white petals floated beneath the cherry trees, the air to-day was a-flutter with living wings. Along the short stretch of road, all the Large Tortoiseshell butterflies in the district seemed to have gathered. In one spot, a couple of them gambolled about a dandelion root, fluttering round and round, and poising upon the yellow pollen-dusted flowers to show off the rich golden-brown and black markings of their quivering wings. A little farther on, a bevy of five sported among the cherry boughs; and farther still there were more, and yet more – in all, more than a score of these not very common insects within the space of a quarter of a mile.

How they danced upon the air, the sunshine reflected in the sunny tints of their wing-colours, their movements so buoyantly joyous and their ordered dance so regular that it would have been easy to imagine they had come together deliberately after their long hibernation to celebrate the coming of May. But, in sober fact, a far more serious motive was responsible for the assembly. These were, all of them, last year's butterflies, which had slept the winter away in sheltered crannies, preserved by Nature for the express purpose of continuing their race: and now they had come from far and near about the countryside to lay their eggs upon the wild-cherry trees, that the offspring they would never live to see might find suitable food when the caterpillars emerged from the eggs.

The caterpillars of the different butterflies are all of them choice feeders. Many kinds can live upon one plant only; the common stinging-nettle, for instance, is the first necessity of life to the caterpillar of the gorgeous Peacock – and it must be genuine stinging-nettle, too; the flowering nettles will not do. Then the caterpillar of the Brimstone butterfly can eat nothing but buckthorn leaves, while the Cabbage White, as any cook or gardener can tell us, lives solely upon the crispest and tenderest young cabbage leaves. The great Tortoiseshell is not quite so particular, for it favours the different aspens and poplars, as well as its prime favourite, the wild-cherry. Another butterfly seen much abroad just now is the handsome little Orange Tip. The male of this kind we all know by its white, gilt-edged wings, but the female is not quite so easily distinguished, as in her case a splash of soft grey takes the place of the orange.

This morning, in the water-meadow below the cherry trees, the air was alive with these insects, as they sported upon the sunny air, chasing each other through the cool green of the willows, or poising to rest upon the forget-me-nots at the water's edge. In one place a couple of the males were mischievously engaged in teasing an old white domestic duck which had strayed out on the stream, with all her train of fluffy little ducklings behind her. Keeping an inch or two before her wicked-looking little black eyes, they flicked at her with their wings, and seemed to laugh at the great clumsy bill which quacked such loud threats at them.

But the Orange Tips, for all their elvish tricks with the duck, were not out entirely for pleasure. A little higher up the slope from the stream, dozens of the females had attached themselves to the smooth stalks of the lady-smock, the green-veined white of their under-wings harmonising so perfectly with the meadow grass and flowers as to render them all but unnoticeable, and were engaged upon the same serious business as the larger bronze butterflies in the cherry boughs. Upon stalks of other flowers of the same plant deposits of their eggs could be discerned, and, in a week or two, when the pale mauve flowers have given place to long, narrow green seed-pods, there will be dozens of small green caterpillars, very similar in colour and shape to the pods themselves, to be found upon the lady-smocks. These in turn will become the new generation of this year's Orange Tips, when that which danced in the May sunshine is no more.

In the midst of a tussock of rushes which stands out from a small island a few feet from the streamlet's bank, a pair of moorhens have made their nest of dry rushes, and every day now the hen sits patiently upon her four red-speckled eggs. If I appear to take no notice of her when I approach, she merely flattens down upon her nest; but, let me once turn my head in her direction, and she slides into the water upon the opposite side with a "Plop!" and away with a lengthening wake of ripples.

It is the same with all birds and most wild animals. One may observe them as long as one likes, providing the head is slightly averted and some pretence of walking kept up; but, once pause, or look full-faced upon them, and they take fright immediately.

Some birds, however, are not nearly as shy as they are supposed to be. From the group of poplars which overhangs the bridge which carries the main London to Portsmouth road across the stream at a point near the cherry trees, the song of the nightingale may be heard any fine evening now.* Why the birds, generally supposed to love seclusion, should elect to sing night after night in the accompaniment of motor horns and the grinding of lorry wheels, when there are romantic woods and glens within a few hundred yards, is a mystery. One probable solution is that they, or rather their ancestors, were in possession of the spot centuries before there was a bridge or even a road there; for the nightingale is a conservative bird, and where it is known now it has usually been known for as long as human memory goes back. But that does not explain upon what principle the haunts they hold so tenaciously to were selected.

As a general rule, the nightingale is fairly well distributed in Surrey, Sussex, and Hampshire; yet, within these favoured counties, there are certain places where it is never heard, though climate, scenery, and other conditions appear exactly the same as in the more favoured spots. One of their haunts around Peverel is the bridge upon the main road already mentioned; another is an orchard in the middle of the village, and yet another the trees about a green upon which an inn and several cottages stand. Between these well-defined spots they are never heard. But where they are known to dwell they may be depended upon; not one evening passes during their short singing season but one of them may be heard and seen, silhouetted against the dark sky, head thrown back and bill wide open, pouring out its heart in passionate song . . .

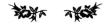

---

*A few hundred yards north of the railway bridge over the A3 south of Liphook.

June

*J*une

*F*ROM THE PINEWOOD in the long, still afternoon comes the soft "Coo, Coo!" of the wood-pigeon. Upon the sun-baked heath linnets flutter from bush to bush, waiting until, had I a pinch of salt, I could put it upon the tails of them, then flying off to the next one and waiting again.

The small blue butterfly has made its appearance, too, floating in little flocks above the heather, or dropping down and threading themselves, six or eight at a time, in silhouette upon a drooping bent, until they look like some new and strange flower unknown to botany.

Of human life upon the heath there is scarcely any. I walk there for days together and meet nobody; but I do not think Peverel was always so sparsely populated. To the discerning eye there are many traces of the occupation of man, from the arrow-heads of the Stone Age to the half-filled trenches of Kitchener's Army.

There are paths and cart-tracks, too, without number; some of them still in occasional use, but most of them overgrown and deserted. Some have been so long disused that pine trees have sprung and come to full stature between the still clearly-defined cart ruts.

Sometimes I follow those deserted paths, winding in and out to skirt the hills and the marshes, just as they were first trodden by the naked feet of primitive man. Sometimes they end in the tawny, bramble-grown cliff-face of

a deserted gravel or sand pit. This is a happy hunting ground for the lover of wild life. At one's approach rabbits scutter; just a glimpse of a white tail, and that is all of them. Lizards dart behind sand-heaps; sometimes a hen pheasant whirrs up and takes wing, leaving her dozen or more light brown eggs to their fate. But at one I came upon yesterday there were no such sights or sounds of sudden flight.

The reason was soon apparent. Rounding the cliff suddenly, without sound, I came upon a happy family party. Basking full length in the sun lay a mother-fox, her warm reddish-brown coat a shade or two darker and deeper than the sand hill behind her. Around and above her, in playful pursuit, tugging her ears and brush, and romping over her just as though she had been a feather bed, sported her two bright-eyed, prick-eared little cubs. The father of

the family sat upon his haunches some yards apart; such childish games were, apparently, not for him. His back was towards me, but I did not think it advisable to reprove him for his lack of manners. Instead, I turned discreetly, and retreated as silently as I had come.

Often the deserted paths led to an open square of green enclosed by a low turf wall. Sometimes a few grey stones are scattered around, or a gnarled old fruit tree, bending before the upland winds, still stands to testify that there, where only the rabbit burrows and the lark drops to earth, men were once born and lived and loved and died.

One ancient landmark I miss upon my return, for the elm tree which marked the end of my small demesne crashed in the March gales and lies, a fallen giant, across the little lawn by the brook at the bottom of the garden.

Why that should have fallen when older and already decaying trees in more exposed situations stood firm is a mystery, for it seemed in the very pride of its strength and good for another century at least. So full of strength that it has bloomed its small green butterfly blooms and burgeoned to full leafage with its roots in the air.

That is the way of the elm. It is a noble tree in life and a serviceable one in death; but it should never be planted beside a thoroughfare or near a human dwelling, for it has a bad habit, almost malicious seeming, of dropping more or less of itself to earth without warning or apparent cause. Our Saxon ancestors knew this. "Elum whych hayteth man", they called it, and regarded it with superstitious fear . . .

Those who go to the country in search of quiet should not go in June. It is the noisiest month of all the year there. At the first peep of sunrise such a gurgling and bubbling of bird-song goes up from tree and hedgerow that every separate twig seems alive.

The cuckoo does not wait for sunrise, but starts calling in the first early greyness, beginning the day as it means to go on until the tardy summer dusk has fallen. As the longest day approaches it calls almost incessantly, as though it had a certain amount of "cuckooing" to get through, and was much behindhand with the sum of it. In its extreme haste to finish and depart overseas it falls into a kind of eager stammer – "Cuck-cuck-oo!" instead of the clearly enunciated "Cuckoo!" of a month before.

The song-birds, most of them with at least one brood put out in the world, allow themselves an interval for rest and thanksgiving before settling down to their midsummer muteness, and make a second Spring of the middle weeks of June.

The chorus of the older birds is swelled by the tentative chirps and trills of the new generation. The young blackbirds especially are apt pupils, fluting the sweet, full notes over and over in exact imitation of their parents. Away in the distant and lonely recesses of the heath, whole families of young linnets flit among the gorse. Their new-found notes, if somewhat shrill and feeble, are very sweet. Already they are acquiring the tone of protesting pathos which seems natural to all heath-bred birds.

Nearer home, fat young thrushes scratch beneath the shrubs and gurgle their satisfaction with what is to be found there. Even the newly-fledged house-sparrows keep up a continuous "tweet! tweet!" and as to the young starlings, they are as noisy as their elders, and that is saying a good deal! . . .

It is dark so late and light so early that all through the night there is a glow in the sky; and in the scented half-dark, when cool night winds are abroad, and white flowers glimmer quite visibly from an upper window, it seems a waste of opportunity to go to bed at all. Even the eerie cry of the screech-owl, so blood-curdling to those accustomed only to the lullaby of trains and steam whistles, is welcomed by us as an excuse to play truant from bed by the open window for ten minutes.

There are other winged things besides nightingales and bats abroad these summer nights. Moths, so silent and ghostly they can scarce be distinguished from the petals of white flowers, float here and there about the garden beds. All day they have each of them slept in some tiny crevice, under stone or leaf, or between the furrows of some rough-barked tree. At night they awake and seek nutriment for themselves, performing at the same time their allotted task in the scheme of things by fertilizing night-blooming plants.

The moth is a creature little considered except by collectors. Butterflies are known to all; yet there are many more species of moths than of butterflies in this country, and the study of their dim, mysterious lives is most fascinating.

A common sight at this time of year is the Ghost Moth, which hovers above the fields and hedges at dusk – at one moment a pale, floating shape flitting across our path, then suddenly vanishing. It is usually still within reach of our hand, although invisible, for it has only to alight and fold its wings to disappear in the half-light. The upper side of its wings is mealy-white and glimmering; the lower side, coming into view when poised, a most perfect disguise of brownish grey.

Some of the day-flying moths are so royally marked and richly coloured as to pass with the casual observer for butterflies. The difference can readily be distinguished by the shape of the body. The butterfly has a waist like a wasp, the moth has none.

The nightingale has sung nearer to my door this year than ever before, and I have felt duly honoured; but the song that will live in my memory as the voice of this particular spring is not his, but that of the blackbird which has fluted away through rain and sun since the fairest mild days of February.

Last year, I remember, the garden was haunted by this or another pair, and they sweetened the summer for me in a similar way; but this year the song is fuller and more sustained. If the singer is the same, he has practised his art to some purpose.

Last year, although I searched high and low, I could find no nest, and rashly concluded that the cock bird was alone, and sang for the pure artistic joy of it – a theory that was laughed to scorn by my naturalist friend. He was right, of course. These men of science always *are* right! In Autumn, when the leaves were scant, and pear-picking was in progress, the nest was found, most cunningly concealed, in the main fork of the pear-tree.

This year they have chosen a more accessible site in an ivied stump beside the brook at the bottom of the garden. By leaning over as I passed I could look down into it and could see the five speckled greenish-blue eggs, then the soft brown back of the brooding mother. It is cold and empty now; the young birds, after chirping and hopping about the garden for days, have left to seek their fortunes elsewhere. Yet the cock-bird does nothing but practise his notes all day; his mate, in her rusty brown, so homely beside his burnished black and beak of gold, cracks snails upon a stone for her lunch in the most leisurely manner. Of the second brood, which all good householders in bird-land should be thinking of, there is no sign . . .

How many separate perfumes go to make up what we describe as "the scent of new-mown hay" would be difficult to say. First and foremost, of course, is the scent of the hay itself, the sweet vernal grass, which forms the basis of most grass-seed mixtures. Then there are the clovers, white and red, and the wild rose scent from the hedges which hem the fields in, and the scent of the earth with the heavy dews of June upon it, and perhaps a breath of cottage garden flowers, and a suspicion of the margin of the rapidly shrinking  brook, and the breath of the cows in the neighbouring field, forming altogether a compound of perfume which any exile would recognise immediately as "England in June".

This is the flowering time of the grasses. Along the hedges, tall beads of the brome grass hang out drooping green plumes, each spikelet of the cluster suspended at the end of a slender stem, after the fashion of an oat head. There is the millet grass, too, growing a little lower on the bank, the dark, feathery plumes of it so delicately graceful that no wild-flower bouquet is complete without its finishing touch.

Between the ruts in the cart track below, the tough and hardy darnel puts up a trampled head or two. This darnel, or rye grass, is everywhere; scarcely a roadside or waste place in the whole country could be found without it. Children in the South of England tell their fortunes upon the flat, ladder-like spikelets: "Tinker, Tailor, Soldier, Sailor, Rich man, Poor man, Beggarman, Farmer."

This humblest of all flowering things has an extraordinary power of adapting itself to physical conditions. Upon paths and other places where it has intruded it lies close to the earth, as though to attract as little attention as possible. In waste places, such as undeveloped building land, it ventures a little higher; and, when sown with other seeds for hay, it puts up a long, slender stem and bears its usually despised head proudly, as though fully conscious it is being of use in the world.

Among the roadside grasses, too, are the wall barley and the meadow barley, the flowers of which are easily recognised by their resemblance to the grain they are called after; and a score of other varieties, besides, each one of them as carefully designed and finished as the lily or the rose.

The study of these humbler flower forms will well repay the little trouble it costs. Learn to distinguish the commoner kinds by name, and a friendly face peeps out wherever we go...

Out in the lanes and upon the open heath the broom in flower is a glorious sight. Upon Peverel there are large, long-established thickets of it, almost tree-high, in which the most dejected bachelor, if bachelors do, as Shakespeare said, "love the broom thickets", might sigh his heart out without being seen.

All down the tough, dark stems the pea-shaped blossoms hang, like a myriad of golden butterflies poised for flight. So closely are they set upon the almost leafless twigs that the tall, slender boughs show pure gold against the sky. Seeing them sway temptingly in the lightest breeze, it is easy to under-stand the taste of that young prince of England who loved, when hunting,

> "To bind upon his forehead for a plume
> A branch of blossomed broom,"

and by so doing gave the name of Plantagenet to his house.

It is to be hoped that he plucked his golden plume off and discarded it when he entered the palace. If not, we may be sure that the moment he laid it aside some hireling would seize and rush outside with it, lest the castle well should run dry, or the new brewing of ale turn sour. Even the Queen herself, had she seen it, would probably have tumbled it through the nearest loophole; for, as the first housewife in the land, she would certainly hold the golden flower in particular dread. At ordinary times the stiff, pliable twigs of the plant were cut and bunched together to make brooms, and castle as well as cottage was swept by them; but while it was in flower not a twig was cut, for had it not been said

> "If you sweep the house with the
> blossomed broom in May,
> The goodman of the house you are
> bound to sweep away"?

And, however desirable such a proceeding might appear as a temporary measure, on such as brewing, baking, or spring-cleaning days it would never have done to have risked making the clearance final!

Why such a bright and beautiful flower should have had such a sinister reputation it is difficult to guess. Perhaps it was that it was reputed to be one of the unfortunate flowers which betrayed Our Saviour when on earth. The legend says that once, when hard pressed by His enemies, He took refuge in a broom thicket. The popping of the dry pods revealed His hiding-place, and ever since the broom has been held unlucky.

The actual flower of the broom, growing, as it does, and making its effect in masses, is seldom noticed singly. It is well worth examination. In shape it resembles both the laburnum and the gorse, but its gold is both deeper and brighter than either. Its mechanism is marvellous. The half-opened bud is so arranged that the weight of the first visiting bee bursts open the two wing-shaped top petals and, releasing a spring, discharges a puff of pollen-dust into the air. After that the store is open to all comers, and many a gold-dusted bee emerges to carry the fertilising dust from flower to flower.

To-day, for the first time this season, the long-drawn "Creak! Creak!" of the reaping machine has floated up from the valley fields. It will go on at intervals for the rest of the summer – first the hay, then stray crops of oats and rye, then the true harvest of the wheat. The sound, though harsh in itself, is pleasant to country dwellers, for it is one of the voices of summer, and speaks of long days out of doors, of cool frocks and strawberry teas, and evening bathing in the lake for the schoolboys of the household. In the suburbs the sound of the lawn-mower takes its place – that, and the cool swish of the garden hose, with lighted, uncurtained windows, and a piano tinkling from one of them. The scent of newly-cut grass brings back such scenes to us all, and, whether in town or country, the sensation is delicious.

The particular field beneath Peverel which they have cut to-day is always the earliest in the district to ripen. It is a field, as the farmer himself admits, "made on purpose for hay". Sheltered, yet sunny, well drained, yet well fed by the stream at the bottom of its slope, even in a poor year it can be depended upon for a moderate yield. This year, owing to the much-abused rains in May, the crop is excellent.

All day the two horses, yoked abreast, the one brown, the other white, have tramped the field in an ever-narrowing circle. All day, with a soft swish, long grasses, sweet-scented herbs, and succulent clovers have fallen into long swaths. To-night, with the dew upon them, and the blue mist of evening rising from the stream below, the scent comes divinely sweet.

To human country dwellers, even to those who have no hand in it, the cutting of the first hayfield is a mildly pleasing event. To some of our fellow creatures it is a cataclysm. Each time the great machine, long, keen knives outstretched, has lumbered, like a chariot of death, around the field, lives have been lost and whole families ruined. Last night the long, waving grass was populous with contented creatures; to-night the dead strew the stubble, and refugees crouch terror-stricken in the hedges fields away.

The first sound of its revolutions this morning must have struck terror into the hearts of the more intelligent householders. "Those awful knives, and my eggs not out!" the partridge with the late brood would cry. "And my poor babes, so weak and helpless!" would moan the mouse. Such loving hearts would remain as long as they dared – the partridge wheeling above her nest until all hope was lost, the mouse either perishing with her children or carrying them one by one in her teeth to safety. Other and unattached creatures which happened to be upon the outer margin of the field would make a dash at once. Mice would steal away; rabbits would flee like the wind across the open, scramble through the first hedge, and be gone; old, warty toads would hop off, eyes fixed straight in front, unconcerned in demeanour as is their wont, only the throbbing of their pulses, visible through the semi-transparent flesh, witnessing to the terror within. Those deep in the field would shrink with the weak and timid to the centre, saving their lives for the moment to lose them at the final massacre.

As the outer circle of cut swaths widens, and the inner one of standing grass is reduced to the size of a large flower-bed, the farmer and his sporting friends arrive with their guns. The driver of the machine dismounts; a following of idlers and small boys appears from nowhere in particular, and all proceed to beat the circle of standing grass with sticks. A hare dashes out; a covey of young partridges; a couple of leverets; rabbits by the dozen; smaller things, too; rats, mice, snakes, lizards, everything expected and unexpected.

The principals devote their attention to the rabbits. "Pop! Pop!" go the guns, and the farmer and his friends are provided with rabbit pies for a week. The driver is presented with a couple; if the bag is particularly good, even the idlers come in for something to supplement their dole.

The partridges are sacred until September; no one dreams of violating that unalterable decree of the Game Laws. The small birds mount upon tiny, weak wings, fly a dozen yards, and then find cover in a ditch.

While the excitement of the shoot lasts the smaller creatures stand not upon the order of their going. Mice scuffle off through the clods; wise old frogs hop a few paces, then lie low and trust to protective colouring; the grass-snake becomes one long ripple of speed; and, if no small boys were present, the rate of mortality amongst the unedible would be low. As it is, such things as are seen are pursued with sticks and stones, and the best wish one can have for such innocent things is that school may not be out when their particular field is cut.

The gamekeeper, when he strides over the field afterwards, curses the machine and all its works as heartily as the victims themselves might do if they could speak. Upon the crest of a long ridge of the newly-cut hay are the mangled remains of a covey of young partridges: five small, down-covered corpses, all hacked and bleeding from the knife. Had the driver happened to have seen them in time, he would have dismounted and done his best to save them. In another part of the field he did manage to save a whole sitting of eggs for the mother bird. Seeing her circling flight, and hearing distress in her voice, he stopped his work and parted the grass, found her precious dozen, and

guided his machine to leave her nest intact on a small island of its own. The horses had scarcely started again before she was back on her eggs; and all day since she has never left them, sitting tight within her thin veil of green bents, and following the reaper with bright, anxious eyes every time it passed her corner.

Now it is night, and the scent of the new-mown hay mingles with that of the garden flowers; birds flutter home, and above the woods by the Hermit's Pool hangs one bright star. Looking down on the valley field, with its mounded swaths, one might surmise that no disturbing element could ever enter so peaceful a scene. Men have gone home to their substantial tea-supper; the reaper, with its bright, keen knives, stands covered with its

tarpaulin in a corner; the survivors sink to rest in hedgerow and sandy burrow. And so ends one of the small, unconsidered tragedies of the year...

This morning, four little robins sat perched in a row upon the top bar of a field-gate. They were evidently out for flying practice, but they could not make up their minds to venture, and, balancing themselves precariously, hesitated and cheeped, and cheeped and hesitated, fearing as much to trust themselves to the air as timid children do to the sea at first bathing. They were so young that they had not even been promoted to scarlet waistcoats, and wore only the faintest flush of red on their soft grey neck-feathers, but they had already the robins' friendly confidence in man.

These few quiet weeks before the hay is cut are the young birds' schooldays. Not only have they to learn to fly and to try over their first tentative notes of song, but they must also master the more difficult art of living. Their parents, having launched them from the nest, have turned to other interests; and Nature, having provided the hedgerows with so many young birds that even if a few do perish of cramp, get eaten by cats or stoats, or fall from the boughs and break their tiny necks, it will not matter much, has turned them over to that harsh old school-mistress, Experience.

Under her method of teaching by cuffs and blows, they must learn to distinguish an enemy from afar, what to eat and how to obtain it, and how to secure a warm and sheltered nook against storms and the cold night air.

It is well for them that their parents began to think of choosing a site for their nest in the dark and dreary days of the early months, for the whole summer is not too long for them to master all they have to learn, and if the old birds had waited until the weather was warm and pleasant for nest-making the young ones would be ill-prepared to face the winter when it came...

Just as for two-thirds of the year man turns instinctively to fire for comfort, so for the remaining third water has some deeply-rooted natural lure for him. What could be more refreshing in these warm June days than the gurgling of a running brook over its pebbles and miniature waterfalls? Then, a little later, when the really hot weather comes, there are the deep, still waters of lakes, or the revivifying plunge and roar of the sea.

About a hundred yards from the footbridge in the hayfield this little stream falls over a disused mill-race into a deep and sequestered pool surrounded by crumbling brickwork. It is a cool and silent spot, removed from the road and surrounded by forest trees, so out of the world that it is seldom visited, excepting by a stray angler or two at long intervals. The Ordnance Map shows it as "Somebody or other's Mill Pond", in reference, probably, to the first of the long line of millers who once occupied the mill, of which only a few scattered stones now remain; but although, no doubt, it has still somewhere a mortal owner, it has lapsed into a kind of No Man's Land, and there is no longer even a proper path to it...*

---

*At this time the mill at Bramshott was ruinous, but in 1930 a new house was built on the site. This is now privately owned, and called the Old Mill.

In this abode of ancient peace a human being might dream a whole day away without being once disturbed by the jar and fret of the outside world. Lulled by the songs of birds, the humming of insects, and the sound of falling water, the human struggle for existence fades from the mind, troubles and bodily ills are forgotten, and for an hour or two a kind of truce obtains between destiny and the soul. But to the creatures who live, move, and have their being in or about the water the place is no paradise.

To-day, as I gazed abstractedly down at the swaying submerged forest of green water-weeds, I accidentally dislodged a large beetle with my foot. As it struck the water a pair of wide, fishy jaws were thrust up to receive it; they opened, snapped to again, and their owner sank to the bottom again. The beetle's misfortune was the fish's opportunity; he grasped it promptly, and it only remained to wish him a good digestion to cope with horny case and wings.

Farther out upon the water, the mayfly had risen, and through and through their mazy columns the swallows darted with destroying bills. How many of these fragile, gauzy-winged insects go to the beak-full which each bird must carry scores of times during the day to its young cannot be estimated; but every one of the many birds which skim so gracefully over the water must number its daily "bag" by thousands. The fishes claim their share, too; there are continual splashings and jumpings, and a constant succession of widening circles bears witness to transactions too swiftly accomplished for human eyes to observe. Yet the insects dance on in the sun, their numbers not visibly diminished.

This is the day of the mayfly, and the day of the angler, who knows that, when they are out, the trout will be sure to rise to them, and that, if he baits his hook with a presentable imitation of the insect, he will be sure of his share of the trout: not very large ones in this particular spot, it is true, but plump and brisk little fellows, with a golden sheen on their red-spotted sides, with which any angler would be well content to see his creel filled.

But the mayfly has its own life, unconnected with the trout, the angler, or the young swallow it goes to feed. Examined closely, it is found to be one of the prettiest of insects, with brown and yellow banded body, four gauzy wings, and a group of hair-like appendages at its tail, which, being longer than the whole body, help to give it its light and airy appearance. In its present phase of existence it belongs to that strange order of insect life known as Ephemeridae, consisting of creatures which live only for a day.

Naturalists tell us that the life of the mayfly is not invariably restricted to this short span; it has been known to survive into a second, and even a third day; but, as it has no power to take or assimilate food, it cannot in the course of nature live long. For the mayfly, then, the ordinary problems of life do not exist; it has no food to find, no home to make; excepting for the one serious duty of carrying on its race, it has nothing to do but dance in the sun.

The female mayfly deposits her eggs in a small clotted mass upon the surface of the water, and the larvae, when hatched, drop to the bottom and take up their abode beneath pebbles or in small burrows in the mud. In strong contrast to their parents, they are fully competent to absorb all the nourishment they can get, and to this end are provided with strong pointed jaws, with which they capture and devour insects and other water-larvae.

For at least a year they remain in this state, small, brown, wingless creeping things, living in the mud; then, as their bodies begin to round and harden, they crawl up reeds or other water-weeds to the upper air and wait for the sun to dry and harden the cases which have formed around them. At last, upon some sunny morning in May or June, the final metamorphosis takes place, the shell splits, and a shining-winged mayfly emerges, to dance its one day in the sun, and so complete the cycle . . .

Very early this morning, while the leaves were still silver with dew, the humble-bees were busy about a field of red clover. They did well to be early afield, for there are not a great number of these insects in the neighbourhood, and only their long tongues can dip deep enough to reach the nectar in the clover-bloom, and by so doing scatter the pollen which is to fertilise the plant.

Darwin was the first to notice that humble-bees, not hive-bees, visited the clover fields, and to find out the cause and infer that, should the race of humble-bees die out in a country, the red clover would cease to seed. Since his time his theory has been proved, for, when the clover was introduced into Australia, no native insect was forthcoming to fertilise it, and living humble-bees had actually to be introduced for that purpose. In England, wherever a field of red clover is in bloom, an astonishing number of these bees, drawn

from all points of the compass by its sweet scent, congregate to boom all day about the flowers.

Seen closely, the humble-bee is the handsomest of all our clear-winged insects. Stoutly built and comfortable of figure, clad in striped black and dull orange velvet, its bright wings glistening through its powdering of pollen dust, it goes methodically about its appointed task, never hurrying and never stopping, unless during a shower. It is more peaceably disposed, too, than its relatives, the wasp and the hive-bee, never going out of its way to attack, preferring flight to assault, and, even when driven to using its sting, giving a far less venomous jab than the other bees.

A communal creature, like the wasps and bees, it lives in smaller communities than either, its home resembling rather that of a large family than a city or state. Like the communities of the wasps, those of the humble-bee are built by the efforts of a solitary queen, a survivor of the previous summer who has slept the winter away in some sheltered cranny in wall, bank, or tree-bark. Upon a warm, sunny day in spring or early summer she crawls out from her retreat and immediately starts making a home for her future subjects.

These nests are sometimes made in a hole in a bank, either one tunnelled out by herself, or a disused burrow of a field-mouse or other small creature. Sometimes they are upon the surface of the ground, covered only with dead leaves or other debris, for in England we have no less than eighteen species of humble-bee, and their methods vary a little. Whichever form is preferred, the queen only waits to scoop out a sufficient space to accommodate herself and the eggs from which her first generation of workers will proceed; she then flies off to collect the pollen, nectar, and other vegetable substances necessary to manufacture the wax for her cell-making.

Very soon she has constructed a rough sphere of wax, in which her eggs are laid, as well as a certain number of honey-cells filled to the brim for the refreshment of the grubs when they shall be hatched out. The future thus far provided for, she does not rest, but continues to form fresh cells, as well as to provide the first grubs hatched out with replenished honey stores.

At the end of a month or so the first fully-equipped worker-bees appear, and from then on the community grows daily until there are between one and five hundred subjects living and working together under the rule of the mother-queen of the family. Of these, the greater number are sexless worker-bees, whose duty it is to gather nectar, build cells, clean the nest, and care for the young; but a small number of young queens, or perfect females, are also produced, and these, unlike the later queens of the hive-bees, which are stung to death by the ruler of the hive, are allowed to live and lay eggs, and apparently to reign in a minor way under the original queen. Towards autumn a brood of drones and a few large, strong queens are produced, the latter of which are destined to survive the winter and found the communities of the following year.

The coming of summer and the renewed power of the sun have brought out those small denizens of the heath which, though seldom seen, are apt to deter timid people from walking there. About once in the course of the year, always in hot weather, a glimpse may be caught of one of our English snakes basking upon a bank in full sunlight, or vanishing before our footsteps across our path. As every one of our native reptiles is more timid than the timidest walker, it is gone in a flash, too soon, indeed, to please the few who would like to observe it more closely.

If it happens to be an adder, however, it can usually be distinguished by the long zig-zag design which runs in darker colour down its back, something like a set of V's fitting closely one into the other. This snake, our only native poisonous one, never attacks if undisturbed. In the very rare cases where it does so, it is usually because it has been stepped upon, and for this reason it is unwise to wade through thick heather in hot weather. These cases, however, are very rare, for, although the heaths around Peverel abound with the creatures, notably the banks and adjoining scrub around one of the heath ponds, during the years I have lived here I have not heard of a single case of snake bite.

When such an accident does occur, and we read of one occasionally in the newspapers, it should, of course, be medically treated as early as possible. But in the case of a healthy person it should cause no great alarm, for the bite of an adder is seldom fatal, excepting to the weak or elderly.

Very often the harmless grass-snake is mistaken for an adder, but this, though a larger, longer, and more fearsome-looking reptile, does not even possess poison glands, therefore could not harm anyone if it wished. It has no such desire, poor thing, but, like the adder, is only too anxious to get out of the way of its ancestral enemy, man. The grass-snake, like the adder, feeds upon mice, small birds, insects, bird's eggs, or any other animal food that comes handy; but, unlike the adder, the grass-snake frequently takes to the water and varies its diet with fish.

The hedgehog is a great enemy of both snakes. A few years ago a large estate in this county changed hands, and the new owner when he took possession found the garden terraces, long deserted, so infested with adders that he consulted an old countryman as to the best means of exterminating them. The man, instead of making suggestions, struck a bargain. "For such and such a sum I'll rid your place of them in three months." And this he actually did by hiring boys to collect hedgehogs, which he carried in sacks and turned loose on the lawns.

The slow worm, which often passes as a snake and causes quite unnecessary alarm to the timid, is not even a snake at all, but a long, legless lizard. Its confusion with the adder has cost this most innocent creature dearly, for it is not only much more numerous in most localities than the adder, but less stealthy in its movements, and falls a comparatively easy victim to the would-be snake slayer.

Upon the heaths of Peverel the slow worm is specially numerous, and may be seen upon any hot day crossing the sandy paths at full length, or coiled upon some grassy bank to bask in the sun. An even more common sight is that of a dead slow worm lying in several pieces in the dust, for its body is tender and brittle, and a child's blow with a stick will despatch it. Sometimes it will escape the encounter by leaving an inch or two of its tail behind, a misfortune not quite so serious as it sounds, for it soon grows another to take its place.

Such tragedies are quite needless, for the slow worm can harm man in no possible way. The only share it asks in the world is sun-warmth, a few slugs and insects to eat, and a loose stone in some remote spot to sleep under. The most unobservant, too, should be able to distinguish it from a snake by its smooth, highly-polished skin, which glistens as though it had lately been varnished. Another distinguishing feature is that, while the eyes of the serpent family are lidless and fixed in a bright, hard stare, those of the slow worm have lids and flicker like those of birds and other animals.

It is a pity we cannot overcome our prejudice, probably old as Eden, and resist the inborn impulse to destroy any thing which crawls in the dust. The adder, branded with its "V", should, I suppose, be destroyed, for it has the power to harm, though it seldom uses it; but our harmless reptiles like the grass-snake and slow worm, live their innocent lives in places so remote from man and touch so little upon his interests that they, at least, might well be spared to live out their lives in the sun . . .

Under cover of the long grasses by the field-path the partridge broods run swiftly after their mothers, scattering in moments of danger to take cover under weed or briar, or in moments of acute pressure, such as the sound or scent of a dog, taking to their wings in a weak, but presentable, imitation of the quick, whirring flight of their elders. By these forced first flights they escape many of the qualms of the learner, but there is really little need of them, for the mottled light and dark brown of their backs and wings tone so well with the dusty earth that when motionless, they are practically invisible.

Other partridge pairs have still eggs in the nest, for no bird suffers more from egg wastage; and cold, rain, four-footed or other enemies are frequently responsible for a second, or even a third, sitting before a single chick is produced. For those clutches among the tall grass in the hay-field it is now a race against time, for those unhatched when the cutting begins will almost certainly be destroyed, as well as many a brood of chicks of a day or two which happen to be caught towards the centre of the field.

Unless they can fly these latter can seldom be saved, despite the goodwill of the driver, who, instructed by the game-preserving instinct of most rustic workers, as well as by his own humane feelings, will always do all he can to save them. Only too often it is in vain that he stops his machine when a hen whirrs up, and, dismounting, parts the grasses and peers well around, for the very instinct of self-preservation which causes the chicks to trust to colour-protection is now the cause of their destruction. A few eggs may be saved and handed over to the gamekeeper to be hatched out under a broody hen, or now and again a sitting bird is sighted in time for the machine to pass around, instead of over, her nest, when she is left sitting in state on an island of long grass in the midst of the shorn sward.

Generally, in the latter case, the eggs are on the point of hatching, having already begun to chip, or "spring," as the gamekeepers call it, for then the hen, not daring to sit close with her whole weight upon the eggs is in a standing, rather than a sitting position and more readily distinguished . . .

The growing silence of the birds and the shot-silk sheen of the hayfield more than anything else mark the change of the seasons; but other changes, too, are upon us. Though the woods are still in their freshest green, untouched as yet by dust and heat, the first flush of youth and gaiety has gone from the rest of the earth. In the lanes the bluebells have followed the primroses; hawthorn and cherry-blossom have given place to wild-rose garlands; honey-suckle yield their first sweets to the bee, and the cool, sedate elder stands clad in its trusses of clotted-cream bloom.

Down in the water-meadows the ragged-robin paints whole acres with its sunset glow, and the pale lilac spikes of the sweet-scented orchis stand, delicately fresh, among the rushes and tall green "sweeps' brushes" of the horse-tail.

Higher up, in the sunnier, drier pastures, the common orchis still shows a few deep purple spikes where the grass has been kept cropped by grazing cattle. A romantic name given to this common orchis in the South is that of Danes' Blood, because it is said to have been formerly supposed that wherever it grows the blood of these, our foemen of a thousand years back, was spilt.

If this were so, England must have run red from end to end, for the common orchis is found in every damp meadow throughout the South and Midlands at least. It is an interesting coincidence, however, that fringing a little bay in the Isle of Wight, at a spot where the Danes must certainly have landed on their constant raids upon Quarr Abbey and the infant town which is now Ryde, the grass is still purple in spring for an acre or so with the flowers which always seem to have a redder tinge there than elsewhere.

In a few favoured spots up and down the country the wild lily-of-the-valley is now blooming. One such spot I know in the Midlands, far from roads in the depth of a wood of most ancient timber, where the cool green and delicate lily-bells make a perfect paradise in the sequestered shade.

I came upon them unexpectedly in my youth at sunset after rain on a June evening, and can never forget that moment's impression. Hemmed in by the deep greenery, sparkling with raindrops at each bell's tip, filling the air with perfume, they seemed more than mortal flowers. And more than mortal, too, seemed the voice of the only other beholder, a blackbird which sang on and on through the deep silence – such ecstasy in his voice, such pain, as of loveliness too fair to bear looking upon.

July

July

*T*HE TURN OF the year has come; one feels it just as surely and distinctively as the rising of the sap in February, the burgeoning of spring to summer in later May.

In the woods, the foliage has deepened to a sober and uniform green; the cool, deep leaves, layer upon layer, turn aside the pattering drops of the summer shower or interpose a solid canopy of shade against the brazen sky of noon. Gone are the tender and variegated hues of spring, the young green of the beech, the golden-bronze of the oak shoots, the tapestry of wild flowers; only here and there, where the rays of the sun penetrate, does a long finger of gold lie upon the moss by the tree bole.

These green mansions are mostly silent ones; the birds which made music all day long there a month ago are away about their business in wheat field and hedgerow; the cuckoo has gone and the nightingale. Sometimes down a green hazel vista the thrush may still be seen cracking some hapless snail upon a stone, or the sound of the "tap, tap" of the woodpecker comes faintly upon the afternoon

silence; but usually the only sound is the sighing of the wind in the tree-tops.

In the meadows the grass beneath the hedgerow elms is trodden by cattle; they stand for hours together chewing and ruminating in any patch of shade. The odour of them, together with the scent of drifting pollen, gives a kind of sultry sweetness to the air very characteristic of the time of year.

Down by the stream, where the scythe of the hay-mower has spared it, is a natural garden of the brightest hues, gold of ragwort and purple of willow-herb and loosestrife, scarlet of poppy and inter-twining mauve garlands of vetch. Amongst them are still a few cream-coloured plumes of meadowsweet, late-stayers, for their season is, properly speaking, May and June, and the lady-like delicacy and grace of them contrasts strangely with the coarse, vigorous, sunburnt vitality of the genuine midsummer flowers.

The wandering footstep there crushes the watermint, the aromatic, mem-ory-unlocking scent of it, together with the stagnant, yet indescribably pleasant, smell of the shrunken waters proclaim more loudly than any calendar – July! . . .

Lately I have been watching the water-spiders. The study of them is most fascinating; the whole art of the diving-bell was known to their clan for countless ages before man conceived the idea and put it forth as a new one.

Although spending the greater portion of its life beneath the surface, this insect is as dependent upon air for breath as man; but Nature has equipped it better for an amphibious life than she has us. All about its body are short downy hairs; these catch and convey the air bubbles so that it takes down a tiny store of the precious commodity each time it dives. Its fairy freight would not last long, however; so the cunning little creature fashions a kind of bell spun from silky web to form a warehouse, and moors it to the stalks of rushes or water plants by other webs. This done, he has only to fill it and there he is, king of his fairy castle! How often he replenishes it I do not know; but in that silken cell he makes his home and rears his family and seals himself snugly for his winter sleep.

Farther along the bank the brambles make a small and belated spring of their own; the tips of the trailers are vigorous with pale green shoots, and the flowers, starry white and pale purple, promise a rich feast of berries for bird and man. Over the mealiness of the blossoms white moths hover and dip. It is seldom one sees so many of them at one time in broad daylight. I suppose the blackberry season is so short, blooming so late and fruiting so early, that the insects have to work continually to accomplish the fertilisation.

I have heard a great deal about the fertilisation of plants lately, for this summer I have once or twice been botanising with a real botanist, peering into hedges and banks for microscopic and insignificant looking "specimens" and seeing the real beauties of the season passed over or casually recognised by a scientific and unfamiliar name. At last I could bear it no longer.

"Why do you always use the Latin?" I demanded. "You know their own names well enough, and they are so much prettier!"

"Perhaps they are to those people who do not know Latin!" he retorted. "Now this one, for instance," and he stooped to pluck the nearest blossom, "what do you call this gilded Midas of a fellow?"

Had I answered straight out of my own familiar vocabulary, I should have said "buttercup", but I was rather stung by the allusion to my plentiful lack of learning, and wished to show that I knew at least enough to be aware that "buttercup" is one general name for a whole family; so, after searching through the odds and ends of knowledge at the back of my brain, I proudly named it "lesser spearwort".

"Good!" he applauded. "And now for the meaning. The 'wort' shows that it was a flower known to our Saxon ancestors, for that was their general name for all plant life. 'Spear' probably comes from the shape of the leaf. See, it is pointed at the tip! Or it may be derived from some former use as a salve for spear wounds. A whole history behind it in either case!"

"And now for the Latin," I said encouragingly, quite sure in my own mind that it would not prove to be half as picturesque.

"*Ranunculus flammula*. Not a badly-sounding name, you must admit!"

I admitted it freely; it certainly had a fine sonorous ring about it, even if it did seem a little too heavy and gorgeous for the little golden cup already wilting in those strong, capable fingers.

"And the meaning?"

"*Ranunculus* – literally, little frog. Referring, no doubt, to the marshy meadows where it loves to thrive, and little frogs, as the startled exclamation of a certain lady just now proves, are sometimes to be found keeping it company. Then *flammula* – a little flame, a golden flame in this case, over-running the banks and lighting up whole acres. Not quite so ugly and clumsy a name, after all?"

I could only smile and admit it.

Since then I have found that it well repays one to look up the scientific names of our favourites; there is a whole world of history and romance behind some of them. It is pleasant to discern the humanity of the old monks and herbalists who named them peeping out through those stilted syllables. They name them, no doubt, in love and fancy, just as the common people gave them their more homely names.

One other thing my friend told me. Whenever one finds the word "officinalis" included in a flower name it signifies that the flower which bears it was once valued as medicine. "Officinalis," translated literally, means "of the shop", and denotes that the herb was in such common use as to form part of the ordinary stock-in-trade of every herbalist . . .

The first fanfare of colour in the garden has died down. Madonna lilies have taken the place of the tulips; the matted white and silvery-grey masses of the pinks encroach upon the bricked pathway beneath them. Presently the dahlias will usher in the splendour of autumn; but to-day is the day of cool and quiet things, of lavender and mignonette, and the mauves and creams of Canterbury bells.

The one note of definite colour is provided by a thicket of delphiniums, which rise against the willows in the unclaimed waste by the brook at the bottom of the garden. If it were not for that group of chance-planted garden strays, that note of clear metallic blue would be missing from the garden this year; for the drought of the summer before last destroyed all the carefully tended border plants, and their places between the lilies have never been filled.

The delphinium is a flower of the dawn. It is worth the trouble of rising early to see it at its best. In strong sunlight its blue flame pales, just as living fire does; by mid-day it is an ordinary earthly plant of leaves and petals; but in the clear, cold light before sunrise it is a thing of wonder, a mystic torch.

The roses here have a way of opening singly. To-day there will be a crimson beauty, to-morrow a white; for this is a light and hungry soil, unfitted by nature for their culture, and wealthy people who would own rose gardens must first of all import the earth to plant them in. Yet this frugality of nature has its compensations: one single white rose in its own green leaves makes an impression upon the memory which endures for long after a blaze of pink and yellow and crimson would have become a brilliant haze. The flowering season seems to last longer, too. From May until November it is always possible to find a rose somewhere in the garden: a few pallid stragglers last on until Christmas in those years when the frost delays...

Folded away in a valley in the woods, the pool is a world in itself.* At this time of the year it is even more deeply secluded than usual, for not only do the leafy boughs dip down to the water, but fern and willow-herb and reed have sprung in an almost impenetrable thicket to meet them. Upon three sides the usual approaches are overgrown, but upon the fourth is a little grassy lawn, from which Fiona, daring the frogs, sometimes ventures to bathe, and to that I go every day for the sake of the water-lilies.

No lack of life there! The water is as populous as a great city; but it is a dim, mysterious life, very alien to ours. Out in the cool depths below the water-lilies great blunt-nosed carp circle endlessly; in muddy caves beneath the bank lurk cruel pike, waiting to snap their shark-like jaws upon any unsuspecting swimmer-by; frogs slip from the bank, rippling the calm surface; water-rats, breasting the current, make business-like passages from shore to shore. Even the muddy margins where the water is shrieking are teeming with a myriad small and unconsidered living things – water-spiders, water-beetles, water-crickets – almost every land insect has its water counterpart.

---

*Probably one of the Waggoners Wells, near Grayshott.

From the mud of the margin came the dragon-fly, which to-day with glittering wings and sapphire coat of mail is sporting amongst the flowers. The larva of the dragon-fly is a heavy and clumsy insect; mud-coloured, it crawls among the mud at the bottom of some shallow pool. It breathes by taking in the water, extracting the air from it, then ejecting the water again. The transformation of this humble grub to the flash of winged light amongst the flowers is one of the marvels of creation. The Greeks used the butterfly as the symbol of the soul: they might even more appropriately have chosen the dragon-fly! . . .

In these weeks of sunny silence between midsummer and autumn all wild life has a breathing-space. For the birds the great business of the year is over. The nestlings have started life on their own account, and fly in marauding hooligan bands, each one unrecognised by its own parents when they meet. These youngsters have to live and learn; some of them are not too steady upon their feet, let alone their wings, as yet. In the hedges where they roost are plenty of pushing and squabbling, and their first weak, tentative notes are, no doubt, greeted with derision.

For the parent birds life runs smoothly now. Food is still plentiful, food rich and rare for the most part – fat, over-ripe currants which impatient human pickers have overlooked; the last sweet aftermath of the strawberry beds, and juicy snails, clustering in dozens away from the sun. This year, too, there are none of the usual long midsummer flights after water, for the heavy rains have left plenty of pools at which tiny beaks may sip and small wings dip and flick in. If the sun strikes hot, there is deep, cool shade to retire to. It is good to be a bird with family cares behind, and winter privations ahead and unthought of.

It is strange that this time of leisure and plenty should call forth no vocal thanksgiving. One would naturally think that this, not the work-crowded hours of April and May, would be song time; but the fact remains that no sooner does work slacken than song ceases too. The only bird-notes I have heard for days were the soft warblings of a bevy of linnets as I picnicked on the heath, and the full, clear solo of a bullfinch which kindly perched upon a twig, and sang to me while I waited for a bus in a country lane.

It is unusual to see a lone bullfinch. Usually they travel in bands of five or six, robber bands, indeed, for in the course of one morning such a party is capable of stripping a ripe currant or gooseberry bush of every berry. In cherry-time they really become – what gardeners call them – a pest; and often the earth beneath some cherished whiteheart will be found strewn with the stones of the fruit they have devoured.

One gardener I know spent hours in inventing a clapper arrangement, which she roused herself early to work with strings from her bed. It answered for a day or two; then the birds got quite at home with its noise, and would perch and gobble within a foot of it. A sight which so exasperated her that she hurled her best tortoise-shell brush from the window at them, and broke it!

It is a pity the bullfinch has this weakness – if the taste for the fruit we ourselves so much enjoy can be accounted one – for, otherwise, it is one of the most attractive of our rarer songbirds. Its pale flame-coloured breast, hooked beak, and bright, bold eye harmonise well with its strong, clear note; and, although so scarce in some parts as to be seldom seen out of the ripe fruit season, it is as trusting and unafraid of man as the robin.

The one I saw in the lane the other day sat upon a twig on a level with my eyes, and only a couple of yards distant, and sang its song lustily over and over. Even when the 'bus appeared it only flew a little higher in the hedge and regarded the strange vehicle with bright-eyed curiosity.

The 'busses are fully as delightful a feature of country life as the wild birds. More practically helpful than the birds, indeed, they lend wings to the wingless. Here they are a recent institution, and every month now sees fresh routes opened up, and far-away and cross-country villages, names merely hitherto, become places of actual earth and easily accessible.

The printed lists of places upon the routes chime like bells in the memory. "Haslemere and Fernhurst; Milland and Forestmere." What a line of good mouth-filling, ready-made poetry to be printed on the front of a 'bus! . . .

The pinewood in summer is one of the stillest of places. The smaller birds shun the deep shadows and dry, leafless earth between the closely planted trees. At long intervals a jay may flash screeching across a clearing, or the crackling of a pine-cone reveal the presence of a squirrel overhead; but, excepting for the cooing of the pigeons and the never-ceasing murmur of the wind in the branches, those are the only sounds.

The tall, dark pines are very fascinating, bending their heads together and sighing and whispering as though they lamented the constant change in the world around them, other trees breaking into bud, changing colour, and becoming leafless again, while they themselves stand unchanged through the changing seasons.

But, in spite of this gentle melancholy, the pinewood is never gloomy; the darkness of the boughs, almost black in certain lights, only serves to make the sky seem bluer, the sunshine more golden above them. Usually the trees have been planted by man, and the red stems rise in long rows, forming aisles, in which the blue haze hangs like incense between cathedral arches. The very absence of undergrowth lends nobility; other trees rise from a soft mass of clinging verdure, but the tall, slim trunks of the pines spring straight and clear from the brown earth to point upward into the blue of heaven.

The soil is buried deep beneath an accumulation of the fallen needles of thirty, forty, or fifty years of growth. Through the matted mass no blade or frond can penetrate, and as long as the trees stand in close formation they stand alone. Yet beneath the thick layers the earth must be a perfect storehouse of dormant life, for no sooner is a clearing made than all manner of unexpected seedlings appear.

In one place near here a heath-fire of a few summers back ate into the pinewood and left only charred stumps for an acre or more. The first spring after, a scanty growth of bracken struggled through the ashes; then, with the next year, came a thicket of rose-bay, its bright purple of flower and stem vivid against the surrounding darkness, and, very soon, between these taller and coarser growths, tiny gardens of small and tender things sprang into being. In spring there were sheets of speedwell and white stitchwort, clumps of pale dog-violets and small, delicate-fronded ferns; while summer brought the yellow of creeping trefoils, agrimony, eyebright, and all the different crane's bills.

More difficult to account for was a large patch of wild strawberry plants, for, while the other flowers were common in the locality, these were strangers, the nearest growing upon quite different soil a couple of miles away. How the seeds were deposited there is a mystery, for the plants were too numerous and planted too closely to be accounted for by the droppings of birds; and the only probable solution is that it had lain dormant for nearly half a century beneath the thick layer of pine-needles, then, when these were destroyed by fire and the ashes dispersed by the wind, it rose to the light and air with the accumulated strength of the long rest.

The plants flourished and spread rapidly, and this year there was an abundance of scarlet berries among the green leaves. No human being came there to enjoy it, for the pinewood stands upon a hill, an island amidst a forest of oak and beech trees, and is far removed from the beaten track; yet, not one berry was lost or wasted, for the birds found them and celebrated a week's strawberry feast. Tits and thrushes came from the valley, blackcaps and bullfinches from the hedgerows; even the starlings found them out, and came flocking to the feast, and all day and every day as long as the fruit lasted the solitude of the pinewood was enlivened with fluttering wings and the sweet "Tweet! Tweet!" of satisfaction . . .

> "Jog on, jog on, the footpath way,
> And merrily hent the stile-a.
> A merry heart goes all the day;
> Your sad one tires in a mile-a."

The first morning freshness of the year has passed with the gay delicacy of the early wild flowers and the first rapture of birdsong. The countryside is still in its prime, fields ripening unto harvest, apples reddening in the orchards. Not a leaf has fallen; colour has deepened rather than faded, but a subtle change has stolen upon the land. In exchange for the sweet, wild grace of youth we have the staid charm of maturity.

Form has become overlaid by luxuriance. The woods stand clad in fullest foliage, all the exquisite gradations of the early summer tints sobered down to one quiet, uniform green; solitary trees have become great green puffs in the landscape. Everywhere the herbage has spread, overrunning banks and obscuring pathways – even the outline of the hill is blurred by the bracken which climbs its shoulder.

Against this soft dense background of greenery the glowing colours of the later summer flowers seem actually to burn in the strong midsummer sunlight. Cottage gardens are at their gayest with marigolds, asters and nasturtiums; the strong golds and purples of the wildflowers line every lane and roadside. In the hedgerows the honeysuckle has replaced the wild rose, and the silvery plumage of travellers' joy veils the first orange-scarlet of ripening berries. The air is yellow with strong sunlight and heavy with honeysuckle and pollen scents.

About Peverel the latter part of July is a silent time. The cheerful sounds of man's activity in the fields have ceased for these few weeks between haytime and harvest. Many of those who turned the hay a fortnight ago are now far away, picking currants or raspberries in the great fruit-gardens to the south; the regular workers have gone back to their separate jobs about the farmhouse, and the solitary labourer, harrowing the hillside field, has enough to do to guide his team, man and horses alike flagging beneath the direct rays of the sun and irritable from the dust which the teeth of the implement raises in a cloud about them.

Excepting for a subdued rustling through the thick foliage, the winds are stilled. The birds crouch voiceless in the shade; even the water-courses have shrunken until the last tinkling of running water is silent. Only the sharp chirring of a grasshopper cuts the air like a saw, or the crooning of a dove stirs the silence of the pines.

From these familiar, near-at-hand scenes the glory has certainly passed. The roads are dustier than the fields, and unlovely with the holiday traffic; the long grass beneath the trees is dank beneath the shade. Cattle trample the earth beneath the meadow hedgerows, and he who would get to the heart of July must go farther afield.

Most tempting of all, perhaps, to those who can choose is the great open freshness of ocean. It is good upon these hot afternoons to explore the strange, exquisite wild life in some rocky pool, to rest with a book in the semi-twilight of a cave, or, leaving our cares with our clothes behind us, to swim far out into the sunlight, a new being in a new element.

But to-day my readers must be content to remain inland with me, for Peverel is one of those tantalising places where sea winds and sea fogs sweep over the land and gulls fraternise with rooks at the plough-tail in stormy weather, while it is still so cut off from the coast by hills and heath that to reach it at its nearest point involves a considerable journey.

The faint resentment this reflection always arouses was soon dissipated this morning, when I set out with my thermos and sandwiches for a day in the open. I did well to start early, for the sun, already high in a cloudless sky, gave promise of great heat. A heavy dew had fallen in the night, silvering the turf, freshening the flowers, and loading with dew-drops the gossamer threads which already festoon the bushes and lie in delicate patterns upon the grass. A light breeze sharpened the edge of the air and stirred the perfume of honeysuckle.

Early as I was, I had not gone a mile before I met a little band of Gipsy children returning from what we should consider a good day's work. They carried between them great baskets of ripe whortleberries, and each sunburnt face was smeared purple with the juice of other berries which had somehow lost the way between finger and basket.

"Buy some! Buy some, lady!" they cried, dancing like a drove of little wild colts about me, serenely ignoring the fact that I was going away from, and not towards, home, and had nothing but my bare hands to carry a purchase in.

They had been out since four, they told me, and had made good use of their time, for the tiny whortle, or "hurt", as they call it, is the most tedious of all berries to pick, thousands going to fill quite a small vessel.

"And now, I suppose, you are ready for breakfast?"

The words dispersed them like an incantation. Without the formality of a farewell, they shouted for 'Enery and Is'bel to hurry up, and were off at full speed towards the column of blue smoke which arose from the heath in the nearest hollow.

Surely the odour which followed me, mingled with that of the woodsmoke, was too savoury for mere rashers. There were mushrooms in the pan as well, or I am much mistaken – small, pearly button mushrooms, with under-sides pink as rose-petals; mushrooms which their fathers and elder brothers had found when they went to call up the horses. Then, as they tracked their steeds by the long, dark trails their feet had left in the dewy turf, the mushrooms were spied, caps filled, horses caught by the mane and galloped home bare-backed, and the frying-pan was sizzling over the pine-wood fire before decent, hard-working cottagers had finished rubbing their eyes and wondering if it were worth while to go mushrooming so early in the year.

Just where the footpath branches off from the road the rustic double or "kissing" gate is overhung by a tall bush of wild guelder rose. This year the tree is a little late in blooming, retarded, like many other things, by the frosts in May, but during the last week its scores of flat white clusters have opened, and to-day there was all the freshness of the morning upon the pure white flowers and flat, cool leaves. From a short distance the outer circle of large white florets looked like a ring rather than a cluster, for the inner florets are a dingy cream – the colour of a dropped handkerchief against a snowdrift.

I wonder if any other flower is quite such a dead white as this outer circle of florets. The lily, of course, is fairer, but its petals are too glistening and light-reflecting for absolute whiteness, while almost every other white flower has a tinge of cream, of green or mauve or palest pink. Even the cultivated guelder rose of our gardens, in spite of its second name of snowball, retains to the end the slight tincture of pale green which the wild variety loses as soon as the petals are fully expanded.

So striking is this pure white circle against the dark foliage that it comes as a surprise to most of us to learn that, strictly speaking, this outer ring of larger florets are not flowers at all, but enlarged petals evolved, it is supposed, to attract insects to an otherwise inconspicuous flower, and that not the pure white, but the dingy inner florets are the real thing, and responsible for the drooping clusters of bright crimson berries we shall see later in the year. In the case of the garden guelder rose there are no berries at all, for the beautiful, but barren, outer petals have been cultivated at the expense of the fruitful inner florets.

With the rise of the cycle and its later development, the motor-cycle, the footpath way grows more overgrown and deserted every day. Years ago, the footpath rights were jealously cherished. All kinds of people used it; the housewife plodded along with her market basket; the parson upon his parochial visits; children went that way to school, men to work, and lovers, especially, had a fondness for it, as the stiles and kissing-gates would testify if they could speak.

This morning, the only passenger excepting myself was a solitary hare, which came loping up a slope, a tame and rather tired-looking creature, all the madness of March in it subdued by family cares. I doubt, indeed, if more than one human being a week passes that way, for the stiles are rickety, falling to decay, or already replaced by uninviting-looking five-barred gates; while in one or two places where it crosses a field the plough has actually turned up the pathway, not being lifted over as it was in the old days.

At the approach of an intrusive footstep toads scrambled away into the long grass, baby rabbits disappeared with a white tail-flash, and in one place a long grass-snake dragged its leisurely length across. Wherever the path wound by a hedgerow, long grasses, nettles and briars obstructed the progress; tall flowers of the hedge-side brushed the cheek of the wayfarer; moths scattered from the blackberry flowers and floated on the air like animated petals; young birds of this year flew out of the bushes and eyed her more in wonder than fear.

It is a pity that such paths should become disused, for the footpath way is the people's immemorial right, and in the past astonishing battles have been fought to keep open some threatened one. Now they are allowed to lapse without a protest, partly, no doubt, because there is less need of them, but also because they are closed so quietly and gradually that the public does not realise what is happening.

Years ago, if farmer or squire wished to close a path and imagined they had

the right to do so, they adopted high-handed methods; fields were ploughed over the paths, gates shut and locked and barbed wire spread to punish the unwary. Then came the people in a body; gates were thrown off hinges, wire was cut, and those who never went for a walk from one year's end to another put on their Sunday clothes and promenaded with their numerous progeny.

Now a little is taken at a time. A ploughed-up footpath turns back those with light stockings and thin shoes; a five-barred gate with padlock and chain is substituted for the old kissing-gate. Lastly, and most effective of all, a house is built somewhere beside the track, the footpath carefully preserved as the law requires, but reduced to the narrowest and straitest of ways and fenced in with high boards or barbed wire. Then, of course, no one with any manners cares to skirt someone else's tennis lawn, especially when that someone else lolls in a garden chair and regards the intruder as one might a curious and rather unpleasant insect. Very soon, in such cases, the old public way is abandoned to nettles and briars until such time as the law shall allow the landlord to close it officially as disused.

The path of which I am speaking is not in so bad a case as yet. Although overgrown in places, it can everywhere be traced; a brave little way, beaten firm by the footsteps of countless generations, turning and winding and almost doubling back upon itself, but leading at length from one main highroad to another.

At one point my way lay between wheat, tall and heavy of ear and just turning from its blue-green bloom to the yellow of ripeness. Winding between the acres the footpath wandered, a narrow passage through a billowing sea, breast high upon either side. The wind came shivering through, bending the rich ears all one way and ruffling the scarlet poppy patches. Shadows of clouds passed swiftly over, swallows skimmed the green-gold surface and small blue butterflies floated upon the breeze.

Had two wayfarers met there one or other must have trampled the corn; but no such contingency occurred. Not a soul was in sight, and not a sound of man's activity was to be heard save the creech of a railway engine passing through the valley with its freight of holiday-makers bound for the seashore.

The earth at the base of the tall stalks was a secret garden. Heartsease and chamomile, tiny yellow trefoil blooms, scarlet pimpernel and the bluest of blue speedwell all turned bright eyes to the sun when the corn-stalks were parted above them. The pinkish mauve convolvulus cups of the bindweed were everywhere, climbing the wheat-stalks, over-running the earth and providing a feast for a multitude of honeybees.

How magnificently fruitful is the wheat! Each ear close-packed up the stalk with the grain in fours, so thick and full that a single stalk will often bear as many as a hundred seeds. And what a marvellous example of man's patience and skill, which, through the ages, have evolved this great food-bearing plant from the humble grass it originally was.

Although the grain was but half-ripened, the birds were already harvesting. Starlings, already in flocks, flew up at the sound of a footstep, took up their position upon an ash tree in the nearest hedgerow and waited with noisy impatience until the coast should be clear again. The sparrows were even bolder; poised upon their selected stalk they continued pecking and devouring. None of the birds took the slightest notice of the fearsome-looking scarecrow which stood upon tall broomstick legs in the middle of the field, in spite of its complete suit of broadcloth and what must surely be the last top-hat in the neighbourhood.

I reached my destination about noon and sank gratefully down upon the mossy bank of a small pool hidden away in a thicket of oak trees and ferns. How cool and quiet such places are upon a hot summer day, far from the dust of roads and the noise of towns, with only the stirring of the birds in the branches, or the ripple of a fish in the water to break the silence. Even the light has a quiet, subdued quality. It is easy in such a place to imagine one's-self "a green thought in a green shade".

To-day the very water was green, for the little woodland pool was covered with the wide, smooth leaves of waterlilies, each plant with its buds about it, some still green, others white at the tip, with here and there a fully expanded flower – an ivory chalice filled with palest gold.

To and fro among the flowers little black dabchicks played hide-and-seek, disappearing with a loud splash at one point and coming to the surface again a dozen yards away; dragonflies flashed past in their glittering mail; a wagtail took its bath and flirted its wings upon a tiny beach beneath the bank; a timid little willowwren peeped out from a bush, then, at the sight of a human intruder, disappeared as noiselessly as a mouse. The air was cool and moist with fresh-water smells, of rushes, crushed grasses and mint.

It was the very abode of Peace, one of those oases provided by an All-wise Love for man to fly to when the problems of life press hardly, not in order to evade them – we can none of us do that – but to look at them sanely from a distance, and gather fresh strength for the conflict.

August

August

D OWN BY THE POOL the vegetation is almost tropical in its exuberance. Broad, fleshy-leaved waterweeds have grown up, and almost touch the creeper-wreathed branches above. Beneath their shade, red and orange and speckled fungi take the place of flowers; pearly, half-opened toadstools, like rings of fairy umbrellas, decorate the decaying stumps of fallen trees. Even the light filters greenly through the many layers of leafage; there is a darkness, dankness and silence there, which, although not without glamour, is less to my taste than the free air of the open downs.

Yet for the sake of the water lilies, I go there almost daily, keeping paths open which but for me would, at this time of year, not be paths at all. The mystic loveliness of the water lily has renewed its ancient sway over me, lost since childhood. During the years when I saw them not, or saw them only under artificial conditions, I was, like most other people of to-day, ready to consign them to the limbo of bad art; but not all the hand-painted tea-cosies in the shops can spoil the water lily for one who has lately gazed to the full upon its natural beauty. It is, indeed, the "plant and flower of light", as old Ben Jonson says of its sister of the garden.

In and out between the lily leaves glide many fish; roach and chubb and the more picturesque carp. The latter are especially plentiful, and may be seen at any time swimming round and round in shoals in the cool, clear water, like goldfish in a bowl. They are a little like goldfish in shape, too, blunt-snouted and broadfinned; but instead of gold tissue for a dress they wear a silvery coat of mail-chain armour, for every separate scale is outlined.

These fish have been so long undisturbed by man that some of them have grown to a great size; seven, eight, or even ten pounds, I should think, judging by my recollection of fishing trophies I have seen framed and glazed.

Their ancestors did not live so peacefully, for three centuries ago this pond was of sufficient value as a fishpond for the use of it for a term of years to be left in a will as a substantial legacy. In those days, the fishpond was as essential a part of a demesne as the kitchen garden is now. Sheep and oxen, as well as pigs, having, from lack of artificial winter food, to be slaughtered in autumn and salted down, a few weeks of such salt food must have made a little fish a very agreeable change of diet. Friday, too, came once a week, and had to be provided for; not to mention the weanling child, the invalid, or the sick poor without the gates.

The mistress of a country house was then a "lady" in a literal sense, a giver of bread, indeed, and the wheat to make the bread had to be sown and harvested and ground into flour all under her own directions before the bread could be made.

I wonder what such a one would have thought could she have been presented, as I was last week, with a pink and white square of ice cream which had travelled forty miles upon a hot summer day and yet not had time to melt! To make such a delicacy for some special festivity she and her stillroom maids would have worked a whole morning behind closed doors, and the ice to freeze it men would have dragged from the cave in the shadiest part of the grounds, where it had been stored in winter when the lake or the moat was frozen.

Other days, other ways! For myself, I would desire a combination of old romance and modern machinery, for however we may regret the passing of much of the wholesome goodness of the past, no housewife would wish to return to the era when everything, down to soap and candles, had to be made at home, and the hand-stitching of shirtcuffs by candlelight lost to us who knows how many women poets and painters!...

We have each of us our own

particular earthly Paradise, a spot of earth to which our thoughts turn while our bodies are far distant as the one place in all the world where we would wish to be . . .

In my love for my own especial earthly Paradise, human associations play little part. I have usually gone there alone, and the only past it has for me personally is a series of memories – of days when the quivering blue of earth and sky met in a steely line on the horizon; or of other days, when the sea mists shrouded the land and veiled the birches in the little wood tucked back inland; of April days of rain and rainbows, and of Autumn sunsets flaring across the sea.

Two or three times a year I make a pilgrimage across the county to spend a few hours there. Sometimes in spring, oftener in autumn, but always once in August, for then the sea-lavender is in bloom.

Yesterday I stood there, upon a tall, sandy cliff overlooking the Solent. To the east of me, immediately below, the mouth of a tidal river meandered between woods and marshes and sand dunes. Along its banks, overflowing the marshes and trickling like rivulets between the sand-hills, the sea-lavender tinted the land a misty bluish mauve.

It was not so much a colour as a shade of one, a faint haze recalling the middle distance in winter pinewoods, or the fading line of distant hills. In comparison the sea was purple, a strong, deep purple, flecked with the darker tones still of submerged seaweed beds.

On one side of the bay of which my sandy bastion was the centre the low, wooded shores of the New Forest swept in a semi-circle; upon the other, but far distant, were piers and bathing tents, hemmed in by the purple ridge of the Purbeck Hills.* Out upon the bosom of the water the green fields of the Isle of Wight slept in the sun.

*From this spot Flora may have been able to see Peveril Point, which juts out into the sea at Swanage. It may even have suggested to her the name for these papers.

It was a day of blue sky and drifting cloud-flecks, of August heat tempered with sea-breezes; a day when keen, revivifying sea-odours mingled with the scent of the sun-drenched earth. Could a sick person have been transported there he must have felt better; a sad one happier; one who was neither sick nor sorry could scarce have refrained from singing aloud.

Neither sick nor well, glad nor sorry, were there to enjoy it. River bank, shore, and sand dunes were alike deserted. Far away upon the sands a few black forms, small as flies, at that distance, straggled beyond the bathing tents. Between the nearest and me were a couple of miles of sandy shore and wrinkling tide.

Once or twice during the day a sailing boat with crimson wing dropped down the river, tacked, and went back again. Plovers wailed over the flats; sea-birds swooped and circled; larks sprang from the turf, soared and sang, then dropped to earth again. Otherwise I had the whole headland to myself.

It was not always so desolate there. Long ago those sandy solitudes were covered by a Roman city. Delicately-nurtured women, exiles in a savage country, stood upon the spot where I was standing and strained their eyes for the first sight of a vessel from home. Upon the flats by the estuary, where the seabirds were complaining, the word of command rang out to the soldiers of the Legion at drill. Dark-eyed Roman children, already proud of bearing with the consciousness of a ruling caste, played at ball upon the seashore, or hunted for violets in the wood.

It is all gone, dissolved like a dream, as the earthly traces of ourselves will go, too, in time. A thousand years hence, perhaps, some dweller in a new city upon the heights will muse over the ruins of the pleasure city among the pinewoods upon the plain below, and spare a pitying thought to a race which had use for picture palaces and public-houses.

Before the war a party of excavators laboured for months there. The scene of their operations was screened and secluded, as though the pebbles they turned up so freely had been diamonds. The reward of it all was a handful of coins, a few broken shards, and a woman's necklace. That handful of dingy objects upon a museum shelf is all that remains of the Romans of Hengistbury and their city on the hill.

The excavators are almost as dim in the past as the Romans. The sand-heaps they screened and sifted are threaded with coarse grass again; bracken has pushed up through their flint-heaps; even the heather has gained roothold in dark mists and patches upon the sand. Another season or two and the scene of their labours will be undistinguishable from the natural hillocks around.

But, though man has forsaken the city of Hengist, it is still populous. Rabbits in thousands burrow in the sand-hills; lizards bask at their doorways in the sun; the reed-beds fringing the estuary are alive with water-fowl; birds flutter in every bush; insects riddle each sod. . . .

The tide was receding. The sandstone rocks beneath the Head were dark and dripping; the pools were full of stranded things left behind by the sea. The one nearest to me was a world in miniature, peopled by a strange and uncanny life – staring-eyed shrimps, ill-natured crabs, ready to nip the most gentle of investigating fingers, queer flat insects, hiding in the seaweed, and sea-anemones, like scarlet flowers.

Many other living things, strange to me and beyond my knowledge, hid in the crevices of the rocks or swayed gently in the water. Some day, if ever I live near the sea again, I hope to learn more of them, but yesterday I poked amongst them with the ignorant pleasure of a child.

I had not gained my seat among the rocks unchallenged. As I scrambled down the Head, the gulls and kittiwakes protested in a cloud. For ten minutes at least they wailed and circled above me, as though my intrusion was almost more than they could bear.

From the multitude of gulls a stranger might have supposed the sandstone cliff to be the nesting-place of a colony. It is not, but merely a landing-stage upon which the birds congregate upon their journeying to and fro between their home in the chalk-cliff by the Needles to their fishing grounds upon the opposite coast.

After a time they tired of wheeling and screaming, and dropped in a body upon the waves a short distance from shore. There they remained in a close square, the waves white with them, pecking and squabbling over some feast provided by Nature, or discarded by man, for their benefit.

Presently a pair of cormorants winged heavily out from the river, settled

themselves upon two stakes a few yards out to sea, and commenced their toilet. First one, then the other, would open a sooty wing, stretch it to its full width, and fan it gently in the warm air to dry it. Evidently they had been up-river with the tide, and had good success with their fishing, for there was an unmistakable air of well-fed content about their attitude as they sat, alternately drowsing and preening, in the sun.

At close quarters the cormorant is seen more sinister looking than in flight. With its hunched figure, like that of a deformed black giant among the innocent whiteness of the gulls, its hooked claws and eagle beak, it looks the very emblem of evil it was once supposed to be.

There is something primitive looking, too, about its appearance; it seems a survival of some ruder, wilder era. It is easy to imagine it hovering over primeval seas in days when

> "The plesiosaurus plashed among the mud,
> And the fern forest never saw a bud."

In "Paradise Lost" Milton made Satan assume the form of a cormorant, and a superstitious dislike of the bird has survived among fisher folk till the present day. But "to understand is to love", and those who have tamed them declare the cormorant to be of such a high order of intelligence, and capable of such faithfulness and affection to man, as to be only comparable to the dog.

In the east the birds have been trained from remotest times to fish for their masters, and on old pieces of Oriental china may sometimes be seen the picture of one of them being led by a cord, like a dog, by a pig-tailed Chinaman, or fishing solemnly from a crag beneath a pagoda.

In the Isle of Wight they used to tell the following legend: The cormorant, the bat, and the bramble were once in partnership together as merchants. They bought a ship, and loaded it with wool, hoping to make their fortunes. The ship set sail gallantly enough, but never returned to shore. Ever since the bat skulks in dark corners, fearing to go out by day lest he should meet his creditors. The bramble catches at every passing sheep, and plucks a little wool to hoard to replace its loss, but the cormorant goes out to sea, and is for ever peering into the depths, and diving in the hope of recovering its shipwrecked treasures.

Those two strange wild things, of a species I had almost forgotten the existence of, will for the future have a place in my gallery of impressions of my earthly Paradise; for the last picture I saw as I turned unwillingly to go was a path of sunset gold across the sea, and against it two black winging forms, necks and claws outstretched, dwindling, as they made their way to their home in the rocky cliffs at the western end of the island....

The harvest-home, or harvest supper, is a thing of the past. No longer do master and man, mistress and maid, sit down to feast together that one night in the year. Now the farmer entertains his friends to dinner or luncheon, and the labourer spends a portion of his extra pay in taking his wife to the "pictures" in the nearest town. Master and man, when work is over, go their separate ways; the old personal relation has perished.

To those who feel the fascination of the past this may appear sad; but it is not so really for, even while it existed, this surface good will was often but an empty show. Only too often the farmer who had drained his men of their strength to harvest his grain, paying them all the year round wages so low as to keep them underfed, placed before them at the harvest feast such plenty as to tempt them to gorge, and, even as they did so, made a secret butt of them. The men, on their side, cheered and toasted the hated tyrant on the strength of that one meal, and all the rest of the year criticised, if they did not curse, him. Now there is seldom bad feeling between them; the labourer, like any other workman, is out to get a fair wage for his work, and the farmer of the new school is in sympathy with him, and willing, in spite of his own difficulties, to do what he can to meet him.

Yet those old harvest-home feasts created a pleasant warmth for a day. Once, as a child staying at a farm in the Midlands, I had the good fortune to be in for the fun of one.* Such a bustling in the farm kitchen for days beforehand

*Flora conveys this fun in chapter XV of *Lark Rise*. Several of the ideas, and actual phrases, in this article reappear in that chapter, but without the darker references to her child's-eye view of the feasting and overeating.

– such boiling of hams and roasting of sirloins – such stacks of plum-puddings, made according to the Christmas recipe, piled up in the dairy for heating up upon the day – such casks of ale and long plum loaves would astonish any child of this generation.

Then, when the morning of the great day came, what anxious eyes scanned the skies for the weather signals, for the long tables were laid out of doors in the shade of a barn already stuffed to bursting with the corn already threshed. What would have happened if the day had been wet nobody knew, for, as the children of the house declared: "Father always has it fine for *his* harvest-home!"

Dinner was at one, and every man, woman and child in the hamlet was invited, the poor to feast and the sprinkling of better-off to help with the different tables. The only refusals were from the bed-ridden and their attendants, and to them, the day after, portions, carefully graded as to quality according to the social position of the recipient, were carried by the children from the remains of the feast. The only person who could have come, but did not, was an old bee-wife called "Queenie", who was under the delusion that her bees would not work unless she sat in the sun by the hives all day and hummed to them.

At one o'clock, then, the cottagers sat down to the feast. Outwardly it must have appeared an idyll materialised. The tables spread with abundance of good things – the guests in their Sunday best – the master with his carving-knife – the mistress with her tea-urn – the children in their white frocks running hither and thither to see that everyone had what they required. As a background the rickyard, with its yellow stacks, and over all the mellow sunlight of a September afternoon. Passers-by stopped their dog-carts to wave greetings and shout congratulations upon the weather. If a tramp looked wistfully in, he was placed upon the straw beneath a rick, with a plate upon his lap. It was a picture of peace and plenty.

But it did not do to look too closely. People who live upon the brink of semi-starvation do not study table manners. Upon the actual feasting I will draw a veil; suffice it to say that it was a recognised custom in the parish for people to fast, and make their children fast, for a meal in advance, that their appetites might do justice to the food provided. Amongst the farmer's well-to-do friends half-concealed nods and winks went round as waistcoats were unbuttoned and sashes loosened; and the white-haired old vicar, whose own rosy face was a testimony to his love of good-cheer, went about exclaiming: "God bless my soul, it does one good to see them eat!"

He was sincere enough, no doubt; but a child often sees farther than a wise man, and to one child there it seemed the saddest of sights to see people too used to being hungry to behave well when, for once, they had enough.

The games, again, after the feast was over, seemed planned as much for an entertainment for the hosts as an amusement for the guests. Climbing a greased pole to bring down a leg of mutton, or dipping into a tub of water to retrieve sixpences with the teeth, when undertaken in such deadly earnest, were games less calculated to bring out the dignity of those taking part in them than to amuse the lookers-on. Yet it was all well-meant, and when the farmer paused in his carving at the supper-table indoors to listen to the distant cheers for himself of the last home-going group, and ejaculated: "A good lot of chaps! A good lot of chaps!" both master and men, as far as they understood, were perfectly sincere.

Now, with the glamour of the past upon them, we are inclined to look back upon such old-world holidays with regret, and to consider the present-day dances in Village Halls, with their travesty of evening dress and town manners, a poor substitute for the old country dances upon the green. From an artistic point of view they may be; but in individual freedom and independence of spirit they mark a stage upward, and with that for the present we must be content.

Country people, like others, dress and behave to suit their own ideas and taste, and are absolutely indifferent to what may be expected of them by artistic and literary week-enders. Some wayfarer in Sussex wrote indignantly to a daily paper the other day because he had come upon a girl hay-maker in high heels and silk stockings. That is very likely. I have seen a land girl turn sideways from milking a cow to powder her nose! And, although such cases are exceptions, most of our land-workers dressing sensibly and suitably, anyone who comes to the country now expecting to find sun-bonnets and simplicity will certainly be disappointed.

But these changes in man's outlook and circumstances, however they may affect himself, make little difference to the rural scene. The hills are the same, and the woods and waters; his ceaseless hewing and planting, draining and enclosing, result but in scratches upon the face of the earth. Against this unchanging background the lord of it may ride upon a motor-cycle instead of a charger, may walk the hills with a golf club or a camera instead of a sword, but he is the only living thing which changes. The owl and the otter still hunt by night; the rook builds in a tree-top, and the partridge upon the bare ground. The same kinds of birds arrive at the same time each year, build in the exact spots in which their families have done through countless generations, and depart overseas almost to a day at the time their ancestors' departure was chronicled by our earliest bird lovers . . .

It is the time of roadside riches. Strong bright yellows predominate among the wild-flowers, and every hedgerow is aglow with tansy, ragwort, and all the numerous members of the hawkweed family. Beneath the coarse, breast-high growth of those and such-like things, patches of lady-glove shade from orange to straw-colour, tormentil threads the turf with its pale-yellow cups; sunflowers peep over hedges, and nasturtiums spill themselves through cottage palings and overflow the roadside banks.

This prevailing yellow has but one rival. The heather paints whole acres with purple, as the cornfields do with gold; thistles spring hedge-high from the turf; the wild-thyme provides luxurious cushions for the wayfarer to rest upon; rose-bay flares against the darkness of the pinewoods, and every roadside trickle is marked by the purple of the willow-herb. Gold and purple are August's august colours, and every prominent flower of the month borrows its hue from one or the other.

Over this rich display broods a dreamy quiet. The mellow, golden-tinted atmosphere has a soporific quality; the birds, at their trying moulting season, are silent; human activity is centred in the villages and harvest-fields. Two or three buses a day serve to connect one hamlet with another; the rich, for their motorcars' sakes, keep to the well-made highways; labouring people seldom walk out excepting on Sundays, and leisured women of the humbler sort prefer to promenade before the shop-windows of the village street. After the men have passed that way to their work in the morning, the pedestrian upon the by-road is likely to meet with more four-footed fellow creatures than those of his own kind.

But the roads, though silent, are not deserted. The quiet walker will not go far before he becomes aware of soft rustlings in the herbage, the snapping of infinitesimal twigs, and the pattering of tiny feet. As he slackens his pace, and the soft, fine road-dust deadens the sound of his footsteps, one after another of the native population will show itself. At one point a stoat or a grass-snake will slip noiselessly over the bank; a field-mouse, threading its own private by-way through the thorn-stems, will catch sight of human eyes upon it, and vanish in a little cloud of dust and scattered leaves; or a toad, all puffed and warted, will drop from a drainpipe and squat, palpitating with fright, among the water-mint in the dried-up ditch.

A little farther on, perhaps, a squirrel, secure in its own safe position upon an overhanging bough, will remain, quite boldly, to watch him with bright, inquisitive eyes; or a hare will break covert to lop across the road and disappear in the opposite hedge. If the observer is silent and not too near, the hare may not be in such a hurry to cross, but will pause in the middle of the sandy road for a dust-bath, scratching and wallowing, then sitting up on its hindquarters to wash its face with its paws, true pussy-cat fashion.

Perhaps, if the same road is taken upon different days, the wayfarer will notice that the same hare appears to cross at exactly the same point time after time, and, when he comes to the spot, he may notice that a small, dry, well-trodden tunnel pierces the bushes upon either side. Such passages are the animals' highways; the hare uses them, and the rabbit, the hedgehog, and all the different kinds of rats, mice, and voles which have their homes in the hedgerow and the fields within.

When such an opening is large enough, the fox will condescend to squeeze himself through it in preference to taking the longer way round, and towards dusk it is no uncommon sight to see one slink across the country roads. But once a fox has passed that way the hare uses it no longer, for not even the hounds at her heels will induce her to go through an opening polluted by the scent of her mortal foe. The cunning fox is aware of this, and it is one of his hunting tactics to pass through opening after opening and so cut off her retreat.

Many of the smaller creatures seen about the roads at this season are refugees from the harvest-fields, where, at the first sound of cutting operations, every living creature near enough to the outside of the field stands not upon the order of its going, but goes. Others, caught farther in, arrive later, half-dead with haste and fright, perhaps, but safe; while the poor unfortunates which happen to be in the thick of the wheat are driven farther and farther towards the middle of the field for the general massacre when the reaping-machine shall have made its last round . . .

Our south country wheat-fields, small wedges, squares, and triangles set in solid green of hedge and wood, are to professional eyes greatly marred by the bright splashes of poppies, charlock, and corn marigold which delight those only out for beauty. To see wheat in the full pride of its golden goodness it is necessary to go farther north, where the large fields are.

One hamlet I remember upon the central wheat-growing plain of the Midlands, where the farmhouse and few surrounding cottages stood upon a slight hill. For the greater part of the year the scene was flat, brown, dull, and uninteresting; but once a year, for a few weeks before harvest, the hill, with its cluster of buildings, became an island fortress in a sea of gold. Standing at the farmhouse door, one looked down upon nothing but cornfields, the low,

closely-cut hedges between obliterated by the golden tide – acre after acre of goodness, reflecting upon its broad expanse the light and shade of the summer sky.*

I understand that it is so no longer; even in that rich wheat-growing district the fields have been sliced up into market gardens, or widened for pasturage for sheep. The farmer whose pride it was to point out his fields, bearded wheat in this, red in that, barley or oats in the other, is farming those fields no longer. Like many others of his class, he came to a time when he had to recognize that out of his richest harvest he could no longer wrest even the frugal living which

---

*These sentences refer to Juniper Hill, and recall the opening paragraphs of *Lark Rise*. The farmer writing to Flora from Queensland may possibly have been her elder son Basil, who emigrated in the mid-1920s.

was all he desired, and for several years now he has been fruit-farming "down under", as he calls his Queensland home.

From there he writes of orange and lemon groves around his bungalow, of pineapples and peaches as common as potatoes are here, of scarlet hibiscus hedges in place of English hawthorn, of a peace and plenty and a brotherhood between man and man unknown in the older countries of the world. But, in spite of his pride in his new country his heart seems to turn to the old one, for he concludes his letter rather wistfully: "When you get this, it will be harvest time in England. You might tell me how the wheat is looking this year when you write." . . .

Out upon the bosom of the lake the water-lilies are out, dozens of carved ivory goblets filled with pale gold. Here and there a solitary bloom has strayed towards the steep bank, and by clasping some supporting bough it is possible to lean over and look down into it. Even were it possible to pick them it would be a mistake to do so, for the water-lily is a flower only seen to perfection in its own natural surroundings. Taken indoors, it becomes a heavy, clammy, and almost clumsy flower, the only possible arrangement for which is a floating bowl; and even then no ordinary-sized vessel will take more than one, or show even that one off to advantage.

In its natural haunts the white water-lily is perhaps the most strikingly beautiful of all our English wild-flowers, and it is well worth while to take a pilgrimage once a year to see its gleaming white and gold upon cool green. Quite early in the evening the flowers disappear, a habit which has given rise to the mistaken idea that they dip beneath the water for the night, an error which has gained for us those lovely lines of Tennyson:

> Now folds the lily all her sweetness up,
> And slips into the bosom of the lake.

Botanists, however, tell us that it does not do so – cannot, in fact, for the simple reason that, having been originally a land flower, the lily leaves and petals cannot live without air, and the disappearance is due to the "going to sleep" habit which it shares with the daisy and other flowers. As soon as the sun is off it, sometimes as early as four o'clock in the afternoon, the lily folds its sheath of green sepals around its petals and becomes practically invisible amongst its green leaves. . . .

Of hedgerow fruits this year there is unusual abundance. Slender rowan trees bend beneath heavy clusters of orange berries just deepening to scarlet. Hips and haws are also changing colour, and both are plentiful, as are also the

holly berries, though those at present are but hard green little beads of fruit. In the hazel thickets it promises to be a record year. Every tree has its clusters of "fours", "fives" and "sixes", and, as these are already turning from green to milky white, "nutting" is likely to begin nearly a month earlier than usual.

The blackberries are not so forward, as the cold, wet spell at the end of June kept the blossom back; but since then it has pushed forward rapidly, and already there are plenty of early berries to be had, while a wealth of mauvey-white bloom promises a record late crop . . .

Every year at this time the goldfinch appears upon Peverel, and may be seen anywhere where there is thistle down for the pulling, although for the rest of the year it is one of our rarest birds, often not to be seen for months together. Probably it makes a special pilgrimage from the fruitful orchard land just over the Sussex border, and comes here for the thistle harvest, just as some humans among us go "hopping" about the same time. All through August and September it frequents the thistle-thickets, then vanishes with the first gale.

The goldfinch is not a very common bird in any locality, although in many places it seems to have increased slightly in numbers of late. Twenty years ago, no well-kept cottage was to be found without a bird-cage suspended above the pot plants in the front window, and, if the inmate of this cage was not a canary, in nine cases out of ten it was a goldfinch. At that time the goldfinch was an object of merchandise, with a definite price set upon its tiny head, and upon Sunday mornings bird fanciers used to go out into the country with their snares and decoy-cages, and one district after another was stripped of them. Now the cage-bird fashion seems to have died out. South of the Thames even a canary is an uncommon sight, and I do not remember seeing a caged wild-bird since before the war.

Just as dainty in its movements, though not so brightly coloured as the goldfinch, that shy little bird of the wild waste spaces, the long-tailed tit, is another great lover of thistledown. Every few hours bands of ten or a dozen arrive at the thistledown thicket, pause for a time to rest and feast there, then are off again on their everlasting wandering from heath to heath and from hedgerow to hedgerow . . .

It is strange that so hard and dry-looking a flower as the heather should yield to the bees the rich, clouded amber nectar known as heather-honey. There is no other quite like it. Other honeys are good, whether from white clover, wild thyme, cottage garden flowers, or the strange, bright blooms of New Zealand or Java; but for richness of flavour the heather-honey stands apart. Some, born in cities, may prefer the pale, sugar-loaded confection of the multiple stores, but to moorland folk the sweet, dark heather-honey seems the very quintessence of summer – of sunshine and keen air and all the delicious pollen-scents of wild, open spaces.

About the heather there is an old legend. Once, it is said, long, long ago, when England was still British, or perhaps Celtic, a wonderful wine was distilled from the purple heather bells, the recipe for which was so jealously guarded that at last only one man was left who knew it, and he the last of a conquered tribe. Rather than betray the secret of the one sweet of his wild home to the conqueror, who offered him his life in exchange, he threw himself from the cliffs into the sea, and so, it is supposed, perished the secret of the old Celtic heather-wine.

But did it? Was not the heather-wine a special brand of the honey-made mead that played so large a part in the mighty feasts of our ancestors? In that case, the recipe was an open secret which survived for nearly two thousand years, for, as recently as the year before the war, a bottle of heather-mead might sometimes be found in the homes of the older cottagers.

The hard, dry, innutritious nature of its foliage preserves the heather from grub or insect pests. Shelter it gives to all, food to few; but one enemy it has, and that an enemy to the death. Here and there upon the moors a patch of heath may be seen, stunted, sickly-looking, and with few or no flowers. A closer inspection of a plant shows it bound to suffocation in the strangle-hold of the dodder.

This latter plant is a parasite, the seed of which takes root in the soil, puts out a spiral shoot which winds about the nearest plant, disconnects itself from the earth, and for the future gets its living out of the sap of its host. It gradually throws out a network of slender red threads, decorated with clusters of innocent-looking waxen-pink blossoms, and these pretty chains fetter the poor plant until it gradually perishes . . .

Upon the under-side of the fronds of most of our common ferns at this time will be found a rusty-reddish substance adhering like powder. These masses consist of thousands of the spores by which the fern families are propagated. An interesting experiment may be made by raising young ferns from these spores – a simple undertaking which almost always meets with success if the precaution is taken of sterilizing the soil by baking it in an oven. Afterwards the soil should be placed in a flower-pot, well-moistened, and the spores lightly scattered upon the surface. Keep well covered with a piece of glass, and, in about a month, the baby ferns should appear. In time, the young plants may be transferred to garden or greenhouse, delightful souvenirs of our summer pilgrimages.

The butterflies upon the heath are inconspicuous compared to those of our lanes and gardens. Here are no brightly painted peacocks, red admirals or purple emperors; nothing rich or rare to cause excitement or wonder, but tiny living scraps of blue, silvery grey, or brown, which, floating dreamlike upon the dreamy air, tone so perfectly with their surroundings that they are often unnoticed.

Yet, they have a charm, these drifters above the open spaces. The common blue, for instance, on wings of dim azure edged with a narrow border of black, has a habit of flitting in bevies above the heather, or, settling in numbers upon a bent, folding quivering wings to form the petals of a strange new flower.

Even more numerous than the blue is the small copper, with brightly burnished brown wings which glance with a metallic lustre in the sunshine. It is no wonder the copper butterfly is abundant, for it has two or three broods in each season, and so keeps up a constant supply. Then there are meadow browns, and the tiny skipper, and the fritillaries – the silver-washed fritillary, the pearl bordered, the Queen of Spain, and so on through all the list of their lovely names.

But, as these last words are written, evening has come: the butterflies have folded their wings, each one beneath the fairy shelter of petal or leaf, and where a few hours ago they drifted in the sunshine the moths now flit, white and grey and brown and crimson streaked.

Behind the pines on the summit of Peverel the last embers of sunset smoulder; the sky, as seen from the lamp-lit room, is dark violet, and across it a brightly lighted aeroplane threads the long distances between the stars. From an inner room come the strains of a violin played by an unseen musician in Madrid; a night-jar creaks like a rusty hinge from the bracken; and, far away, across the misty fields, the village clock chimes ten.

September

September

*T*HE ROBIN HAS come back to the garden again; his sweet clear little song rings gaily out as he rests upon the lilac bush from his excavating labours in the newly-turned earth of the potato plot. The blackbird had never entirely deserted me the summer through. Although, excepting for a week or two in cherry-time, he might disappear during the day, at dawn or sunset he would take up his old station upon the topmost bough of the pear tree, and pour out his soul for my delight. But now he is in evidence at all hours; has become, in fact, almost a domestic creature, cracking his snail upon my freshly-whitened doorstep, or dragging long fat worms from the moist earth with that tawny-golden bill of his.

Birds of the swallow family are discussing plans for their winter abroad; there is a tremendous twittering upon the roof of the cottage at evening time. But these so-called swallows which haunt the valley and build their cup-shaped nests of white mud beneath the eaves of my house are not, strictly speaking, swallows at all, although of the swallow tribe, but house martins. Their small twittering note is far inferior to the song of the true swallow, which, although small and limited, is extremely sweet, and has a motif of tune running through it.

These I often pause upon my way to or from the village to listen to, for by the road runs a line of telegraph poles, and they thread themselves upon the

taut wires like pearls upon a string. Late in the afternoon, when the sun is low, they appear more pearl-like than ever, for the light striking upward touches each tiny grey-white breast and flushes it to opal.

Their tender, quiet little song, so soothing and healing to listening ears and hearts, is a special feature of later summer, for although they sing a little upon their arrival in spring, they are soon too busy with their nests and young to find time for more than a note or two until, with August, family cares slacken and their voices blend with the golden quiet of the post-harvest earth, with morning mists, stubbled fields, and berried hedgerows . . .

All along the sides of the pinewood, and dotted about upon the heath, the scarlet clusters of mountain-ash berries make vivid splashes against the pale, cloud-flecked blue of the sky. Nothing could be more graceful than the tree which bears them, with its drooping boughs and lacey, fern-like leaves.

This lovely tree is particularly plentiful about Peverel, as it is in most places where the wide stretches of open moorland have never yielded to cultivation. Probably it has flourished in such places, self-sown and untended, from time immemorial, for it is one of our few native trees, and the Romans, when they landed, found it already cherished as a subject of superstitious reverence. In spite of all importations, it is still one of our loveliest wild trees. It is also one of the most hospitable.

In Spring the masses of creamy bloom are a table spread with both nectar and pollen, over which a myriad winged things, bees, flies, and beetles, hover and take their choice. In Autumn the birds have their turn. To approach any single one of the many mountain ash trees dotted about the heath just now is to disturb a whole company of banqueters. The storm-cock is king of the revels; he perches upon some topmost twig, almost bearing it down with his weight, and keeps the smaller birds to their allotted places as he gobbles his fill.

With such lavish plenty, the birds become wasteful. The sandy-earth around the roots of the tree is scattered with mutilated scarlet morsels which have been tasted and cast aside. In a week's time each discarded tit-bit will be seized upon as treasure, for the red rowan season is a short one. However bounteous the yield may be, the birds flock to it and feast with such avidity that within a fortnight of the ripening the trees are stripped bare of berries.

In Scotland, I am told, a delicious confection is made from the rowan berry, but in the South the birds are left in undisputed possession. Excepting for a casual glance of admiration in passing, or the toll of a few sprays for the vases at home, human beings take little note of the mountain ash in these days. It was otherwise once. Our ancestors had a use for leaf, twig, and berry. "Witchtree" the Saxons called it, and never dreamed of starting on a journey unprovided with a switch of it to carry as a charm against evil spirits. And

"Rowan tree and red thread
Hold the witches well in dread"

was a couplet firmly believed in down to almost our own day.

The tree was regarded as especially powerful as a protection where cattle were concerned. Down to the beginning of the last century it was a not uncommon sight in remote districts to see a herd of milking cows turned out for the first time in the Spring pastures each with a budding sprig of rowan tied to one horn by a shred of some red material. No matter how obstinate the cream was upon churning day, when the contents of the churn were stirred with a twig of it the butter came immediately, and was abnormally good.

The wonder of it to our unromantic modern minds is that the dairymaid did not commence operations with the twig, instead of waiting until every man, woman, and child upon the homestead had turned the handle until their arms ached; but, no doubt, the "elbow grease" played its part in the transmutation, while the credit went to the rowan twig.

Above the heather, between the mountain ash trees, flit whole bevies of the small heath-loving butterflies. In one place to-day a flight of fritillaries had settled upon a clump of grey-lichened dead heather. With their grey and brown and silver-splotched wings they mimicked the colour of their resting place so well that only the nervous quivering of their poised wings betrayed them.

In another place a score or more of the "chalk-blue" had threaded themselves upon a long stalk of dried bent, two by two all down the length of it, so that their folded wings resembled petals, and created the illusion of some new and exquisite blue flower.

The mere vibration of a footstep dislodged them, and they fluttered about the intruder and accompanied her in a small, living cloud. Fragile morsels of life, which the slightest touch might have crushed, but each one with a life of its own to live and a definite place in the scheme of Creation...

The finest blackberries I have ever seen grow upon a heath about two miles distant from Peverel. A much-frequented main road from London to the sea cuts through it, and motorists, halting for a picnic lunch, marvel at the exceptional size of the blackberries there. It is no wonder, really, for those particular brambles have had a costly pruning: it took a European war to bring them to their present perfection.

For five years this heath was the site of a camp. Where from time immemorial had been nothing but briar and bracken, row upon row of wooden huts, churches, shops, and theatres sprang up in a week or two. Where only the lapwing had cried or the skylark sung, the drill-sergeant's word of command rang out. The whole place became a populous town.

Tens of thousands of Canadian soldiers sojourned there. One contingent after another arrived, the men often soaked with rain or moiled with heat, and always cramped from the close quarters of war-time transport. There they had a breathing space, saw a little of the "old country", and learned to love it. They were drilled upon those open spaces so flattened by their feet that even now the heather has scarcely begun to grow again. Then each battalion in its turn passed singing along that same main road to its fate.

In the course of these operations such flower and bramble roots as were left were cut back to earth and received a dressing of all kinds of camp residue. When auction sales and motor lorries had removed the last vestiges of the buildings, and a small army of workmen had laboured for months removing rubbish and filling in holes, Nature set to work to heal the scars; and almost the first growth was the long green shoots of the blackberry brambles. The fruit, when it followed, was of the finest – cultivated fruit indeed – and cultivated at what tremendous cost!

Now the bushes are of full size again. Bracken has grown up and filled the rents made by bomb-practice. The heather has returned in waves, a purple sea. Very soon all will be as it had been for countless ages before war broke out, and only the avenue of maple trees the Canadians planted by the roadside will mark any difference between that heath and a score of others by that same roadside . . .*

The black bryony, berried like twisted strings of green, orange, and scarlet beads, wreathes the supporting thorns in places until they are bowed beneath the weight of it. The large, heart-shaped leaves, glossy dark-green all the summer, have turned to every shade between straw-colour and deep yellow, and, altogether, it is one of the most showy of all our hedgerow fruits. But, in spite of its brilliance, there is a sinister look about the black bryony; instinct tells both animal and child that it is too hectic to be wholesome, and, although it is highly poisonous, one seldom hears of death, or even illness, caused by it.

Another dangerous fruit of the hedgesides this month is the woody nightshade, or bitter-sweet. This plant is not a climber, although, its own stems being weak and slender, it often leans upon the thorn for support. Just as often it may be found growing low in the grass, or trailing over a bank. Flowers and fruit may be seen together upon the same plant – the flowers in drooping bunches; dark purple, with bright yellow anthers; the fruit of a clear transparent crimson, and egg-shaped. This plant is rightly regarded as dangerous and left severely alone; it is not, however, quite as evil as its reputation, being only slightly poisonous. The deadly nightshade, for which it is often mistaken, is a similar plant belonging to the same family, but, fortunately, more rare.

The deadly nightshade, or belladonna, is the most poisonous of all our native wild plants. Its wood is stronger, its growth more bushy, and its flowers larger and more bell-shaped than those of its woody relative. Its berries, which appear in July and last on well into the autumn, are dark purple and the size of a cherry. Our forefathers called this plant the "dwale", or "woe tree", on

---

*The Canadian military camp was on Bramshott Common, and even today signs of it can still be detected there. Three hundred Canadian servicemen who died of wounds in the First World War are buried in Bramshott churchyard.

account of the toll of life it took in those days, when it was probably far more common than it is now.

It is rather a wonder that, considering all the "dwale" or woe it has caused through the centuries, this noxious plant has not been rooted out and altogether exterminated. It has, indeed, been driven farther and farther from human habitations and cultivated lands to the Downs, woods, and moors – No Man's Lands, where it is nobody's business to destroy it – but, even so, scarcely a year passes but we read in the newspapers of a case of poisoning through it. As recently as this July a child died through eating the luscious-looking black berries under the impression they were cherries. From these last strongholds it would be an excellent "good turn" for our Boy Scouts to dislodge it as they pass over the wild waste places where it grows on their way to and from their camping grounds.

But these poisonous fruits are few compared with the wealth of wholesome and delicious food our hedgerows provide for man, as well as for birds, this month. For one bryony, black or white, there are at least a thousand blackberry bushes, and a thousand thousand for every deadly nightshade.

There is a flavour of wild freedom about the crimson juice of the ripe blackberry. To the Nature-lover it seems the very ichor of the sun-baked autumn earth, and to taste it after months spent in city streets is a kind of receiving of the freedom of the open air.

Along by the field hedges where the children wander with half-filled baskets and purple-stained mouths, the margin of the stubbled field is embroidered with numberless tiny flowers of every hue. There in the space of a square foot may be seen together the daisy-eyes of mayweed, scarlet of pimpernel, blue of the field forget-me-not, yellow of charlock, and streaked pink and white of bindweed. All these infinitesimal things are freshly sprung since the harvest has been cleared, and the dew which lies upon them all day in the shade is not brighter or fresher than their colours . . .

While the berried hedgerows are asurge with those birds which prefer a fruit diet, and many a pretty comedy is played out among the thistledown, other birds wheel in flocks to glean the last remnants from the stubble, or follow the ploughman as he breaks the soil for the crops of another year. Starlings, linnets, skylarks and hedge-sparrows circle against the blue of the sky in flocks of from one score to ten. When anything worth descending for is sighted below, they drop in a body with one accord, and the very stubble seems to seethe with their fluttering and chattering. At the least alarm they are up again, only to skim the surface of the field for a few yards, then sink again, or to hold council in the nearest tree, shaking its boughs and rustling its leaves in agitated confabulation.

Overhead, in the blue vault of sky, the swallows wheel in ever widening circles as the colder air thins the insect life they are hawking for. Very soon the hint of frost in the morning air will become an unmistakable fact, and then food will fail altogether and the swallows depart; but until that time comes they can afford to delay, for, even should they wake one morning to find themselves breakfastless in England, their flight is so swift and strong that they can make up for it by lunching in Africa.

Other migrants have not waited for even a hint of winter. The cuckoo left us at the end of July, the nightingale in August; and every day since has seen a steady trickle of summer visitors leaving our shores. Although we scarcely notice it, one voice after another is silenced in our lanes and woods: the whitethroat has gone, the blackcap, the willow and reed warblers, and the sweet-voiced little chiff-chaff.

How such fragile little birds as these, flutterers rather than flyers, can find strength and courage to cross continents and seas is a mystery. The chiff-chaff, for instance, seems to make quite an effort of crossing a glade in our woods from one tree to another, and is so small and frail that its very song seems to shake its whole being, and yet it can face the wide skies and stormy seas of a sea-crossing. To a great extent, no doubt, these feathered atoms depend upon the wind, waiting until that from the north prevails, then rising and casting themselves upon it with inspired abandon; and that, perhaps, is why their family has a way of disappearing from a locality, then reappearing at intervals for several weeks at the beginning of autumn.

When their recognised signs of winter appear, the native birds near the coast go with the first favourable wind; and presently other birds from farther north take their places to await their turn, and so on, until all have gone excepting a few stragglers, who make their way to Devonshire and Cornwall for the winter . . .

The orchard this month is a pleasant spot. Through the yellowing leaves peep red and yellow streaked apples, dusky skinned plums, and the rough russet of pears. Much of the fruit has already been gathered, and that which remains is so fully ripe that in the quiet night hours the thud of it falling to earth may be heard through the misty moonlight. Those who go to gather up these "fallers" by day must beware of the wasps which, heavy with nectar and drowsed by the cold edge on the morning air, cling battening to the underside of the fruit, and resent disturbance.

Others of their kind, preferring an animal diet, hover about the garden flowers in pursuit of flies. It is amusing to watch them, the flies so agile and wide-awake, the wasp so heavy and blundering. Time after time it charges into the throng, scattering the flies in every direction, and giving its own head many a hard knock against fence or tree-trunk, before one is captured and borne to earth for a meal.

Sometimes in desperation it turns aside to hunt for baby caterpillars among the herbage outside the garden gate. At that sport it is more successful, as it merely has to hover up and down a plant, examining each leaf until it comes to one rolled up in the kind of tunnel which is the caterpillar's abode. Next comes a buzzing enquiry at each of the end openings as to whether the fine fat meal desired is within, and, if so, the self-invited guest dispenses with farther formality by eating its own way through the leafy wall and proceeding to dine on its host.

But the young caterpillar does not wish to be eaten, and no sooner does it see, hear, or sense a wasp at its door than it hurries forth from the opposite opening and drops, leaving a long silken thread behind as a means of return. The wasp, well aware of what is taking place, follows with all speed, and, if the caterpillar has fallen directly to earth, the story usually ends there. But far more often it happens that it has lodged upon an intervening leaf or glanced off into the herbage around, where it remains safe and sound until the time comes to climb up by its silken ladder again. If only the wasp had sufficient intelligence to recognise this thread as a clue, it might feast upon caterpillars from morning to night; but, although it will go searching from leaf to leaf for the escaped prey, its wits seem to stop short at that point . . .

Another sign of the passing of summer is the hooting of owls around the house in the evening. For months past this bird of night has had its hunting hours restricted to the short darkness, but now, with the shortening daylight, its wild "too-whoo!" comes early enough once more to give the last touch of cosy comfort to a warm fireside.

Some people dislike the sound, and say that it makes them feel melancholy; but, apart from its associations, there is nothing uncanny about it. It is, indeed, a joyful sound, a whoop of triumph, for the owl in pursuit of its quarry is the most noiseless of birds, floating rather than flying upon its softly-feathered pinions; only when it has caught and devoured does it give voice to that blood-curdling scream.

The plumage of the owl is wonderfully adapted to its requirements. Not only does the absence of hard quills, such as those in the wings of partridges and wood-pigeons, make its flight silent as moonlight, but the full, thick feathers covering its body are set in such a manner as to stand out almost at right angles, forming such a protection from cold that it can face the icy wind of a winter midnight while other birds cower half-frozen in the thickets below;

and it is this which gives the owl its peculiar "puffed-out" appearance, besides adding nearly as much again to its apparent size.

For all its quaint, wise look, the owl is not a general favourite; gamekeepers nail its dead body to barn doors; nervous people shrink at the sound of its living voice, while mice and moles and other small game must naturally abominate it. The poets have been particularly hard upon it. "Moping", "melancholy", "bird of ill-omen", "harbinger of ill", are a few of their descriptions of it. Shakespeare, it is true, described its "Too-whoo! Too-whit!" as "a merry note" in one of his songs; but even he makes Henry VI say:

"The owl shrieked at my birth, an evil sign,"

and so preserved a superstition of his day for all time.

Superstition has always centred about the owl. Until quite recent years country people believed that the fluttering and screeching of an owl outside a bedroom window foretold the death of the occupant; though this particular superstition could never have been current about Peverel, where every night, in darkness, storm, or bright moonlight, the owls are abroad. Such superstitions probably arose from the fact that night sounds are more frequently heard by watchers about sick beds than by untroubled country people who fall asleep the moment their heads touch the pillow, and to those watchers, as they sit in the night silence with nerves astrain for the least sound from the patient, the sudden loud screech of an owl is especially startling. Afterwards, if the patient dies, it is recalled as an omen; if not, it is forgotten.

Much of the wise seriousness of the owl's appearance is due to the eyes. They are set well in front, instead of at the side, and surrounded by large discs of feather-markings which add to their apparent size and expression of melancholy wisdom. This forward position of the eyes is a marked feature in birds and other animals of prey, while the hunted in many cases have eyes set well back in their heads – the rabbit and hare, for instance, or the timid wee mouse, which forms the staple of the owl-huntsman's diet.

The bird most to be pitied at the present moment is the partridge, harried from field to field before the sportsmen's guns, or crouching, bright-eyed and palpitating with terror, flat to the furrow in the hope of escaping notice. It is marvellous how nearly the plumage of the flattened wings mimics the earth tints of stubble and clod; but the poor bird seldom profits by this protective colouring, for men and nosing dogs traverse every foot of the field, and it often happens that it whirs up at last from beneath the very feet of an approaching "gun". In that case there is a "Bang!" and all is over – a merciful death enough; but other birds, shot from a distance, often escape with wounds to die a lingering death.

The inborn instinct in man for that kind of killing known as "sport" is one of the strangest survivals among human traits. To the rational mind it seems that the tramp over stubble or moor with Nature at her loveliest might be sufficient pleasure without needing the added zest of destroying the joy of life in a number of defenceless fellow-creatures; yet some of the most merciful men in ordinary life find their keenest pleasure in a day's shooting – the surgeon, for instance, who spends the rest of the year in preserving life, will often take his holiday destroying it upon the moors in September.

It has been said that this love of sport is a survival from the days when man *had* to kill tame things. A man who keeps pigs may glow at old tales of wild-boar hunts, but he calls in the butcher to kill his pigs for him; nobody cares for killing hens, though many have to force themselves to do it. But then, the tame pig is confined to its pen, the fowl to its run, prosaic creatures without the least touch of romance about their circumstances or surroundings, while the pursuit of game does at least take man out from the padded security of ordinary life and place him in contact with nature in wild open spaces, an elemental man against an elemental earth, and to that sense of escape three-fourths of the fascination of sport is probably due . . .

During the last month the harvest has been cut and carried, and over the stubble of the stripped fields the smaller birds wheel in flocks, starlings, finches, skylarks and sparrows, keeping mostly together in huge family parties, but not disdaining to mix at times if anything is to be gained by it.

While these small communists skim the fields, varying their diet at times by migrating to the hedgerow for berries, the rooks make a serious business of

clearing the field of every grain. Up and down the furrows they stalk, digging deeply with their bills for the soft, swollen grains that have been trodden into the mould, coming and going morning and evening like little black-coated labourers. Where the stubble runs up to the woodside the pheasants take their toll, each gorgeous cock with his two or more modest soft-brown clad wives; and all day the wood pigeons flap from trees to stubble and from stubble to trees.

They all fare well, for even modern agricultural implements leave a good deal of grain behind, and the human gleaner disappeared from these parts long ago.* No longer are the family parties to be seen, mother and five, six, or even seven children of all ages, not to mention the baby, sleeping beneath the nearest shade. No longer do they rest at noon, the mother consoling herself with the tea the eldest girl has run home to make, the children playing hide-and-seek in the hedgerow or nutting in the nearest copse.

No more do they trail home at night, tired but triumphant, each head fitted with a neat bundle of "handfuls", varying in size with the bearer's age and strength – burdens which in the aggregate were often sufficient to furnish them with flour for a daily "pudden" through the winter, a pudding which, filled with home-grown apples, or spread with home-made jam, was served before the meat course to take the first edge off the appetite of growing girls and boys.

Puddings do not play so large a part in the countryman's menu in these days; food from packets and tins is much more popular, and to provide this father's wages must suffice. I do not wish to compare the past with the present with any prejudice for either, but, great as the improvement in country life is

---

*Gleaning, or "leasing", is described in *Lark Rise,* chapter I.

in many respects, it seems a pity that the old, cheap, wholesome dishes have gone to make way for tinned and preserved foods.

At a short distance from cottages in the most out-of-the-way spots, surrounded by woods, or miles away from everywhere on the Downs, a dump of salmon tins and jam jars may usually be found, testifying to the class of goods the modern countrywoman spends her husband's hardly-earned wages upon. A generation ago, in the same cottages, the housewife had her own little store-shelf stocked with home-made preserves, including such country delicacies as crab-apple jelly, elderberry chutney and the like; while in some secret nook apart, were her home-made wines – sloe wine, guaranteed by its makers as equal to the best port; gooseberry, "that strong and fizzy as you could scarce get near to uncork it"; good wholesome rhubarb and delicate cowslip.

Other days, other ways. We cannot bring the good old days back, and, if we could, no doubt the result would be very unsatisfactory to our modern ideas. So, not being able to go back, we must march straight onward, and, if we *must* eat mass-made food, get laws passed to insist upon its goodness and purity . . .

My way to-day took me through the woods, then out, over long stretches of heath interspersed with pine-clumps – a district which is still a forest in name, though much of it is the barest of open country.

At noon I rested upon a smoothed mound, still known as Queen's Bank, though few remember it as the spot where Queen Anne, turning aside from the main road on her way seaward, condescended to rest and behold the magnificent herd of five hundred red deer, which were rounded up and driven through the valley for the pleasure of their royal owner.*

The forest was old in Queen Anne's Day. Along the valley she overlooked from her bank the young Black Prince must often have passed with his hawk and hounds in the days when his parents had a hunting lodge close by. And even that older Woolmer was but a section cut from the still older forest of Andredswold, which stretched, a great, wolf-infested wilderness, from the borders of Kent to the Hampshire Downs.

There are no red deer in Woolmer to-day. The fine herd of five hundred had dwindled to fifty by the middle of the eighteenth century, and these were eventually captured and carried in carts to Windsor.

To-day the largest game to be seen was a hare which sprang from its form in

---

*Flora Thompson had read Gilbert White's reference to this event in *The Natural History of Selborne* (Letter VI). Queen's Bank is still to be seen in the middle of Woolmer Forest, about a mile from the Longmoor Road.

a tussock of grass in the middle of what was once a bridle road. All around were the deepest silence and seclusion. Scarce one person in a month passes that way. The blackberries ripen and drop to earth without being tasted; the heather grows purple and bleaches without being seen.

The very earth seems to have grown old there; a heavy grey lichen has settled on all things, fledging the thorns and pine stems and crisping the mould between the heather roots. Only the sighing of a pine, the tapping of a woodpecker, or the sudden loud clapping of a woodpigeon's wings breaks the everlasting stillness.

October

October

AT ONE TIME little boys of eight or ten used to be employed at twopence a day to scare the rooks from the corn with a wooden clapper. Poor little fellows, it was a dismal task! Sent out into the heavy ploughed fields before daylight, with a hunk of bread and a shred or two of fat bacon to last them the day, with no human creature to speak to from morning to night and no means of telling the time but the often invisible sun, the day must have seemed endless!

I remember when I myself was a child one such boy running the whole length of a ploughed field to enquire the time of my brother and me. His face fell blankly when he heard it was still an hour before noon, for he had already consumed both dinner and tea under the impression that a day which seemed so long to him must be nearing twilight. To bribe us to keep him company for a time he carved for us a wonderful death-head out of a turnip, which, with a lighted candle inside and a commandeered tablecloth draped round, was set at night upon the gatepost at home and scared not only the uninitiated but the two perpetrators as well!

The carving of turnips is a lost art. That is a pity; but upon the other hand, poorly paid as the farm-worker still is, little boys of ten are no longer sent to languish all day alone in the sodden winter fields to add a mere shilling to the family income.

Another distinct improvement in country life is to be seen in the dress of the field worker. Gone are the days of tattered broadcloth or shapeless and mud-caked corduroy, topped incongruously with the superannuated Sunday bowler. The younger men dress neatly and smartly in tweed sports coats, breeches and leggings, and present much the same appearance as the prosperous farmer used to do. Manners and morals have improved in proportion: improved wages and world travel during the war have had effect, and the farm labourer now is an intelligent, self-respecting workman, on a level, at least, with the town artisan. The village rustic of the past no longer exists outside the pages of the comic paper.

Here upon Peverel time stands still; the heath glows richly with warm colour, and my sheltered valley is filled these Autumn days with mellow sunshine, like a cup with wine. The trees still stand in their gold and russet and

crimson, not a leaf shed or a colour dimmed, as though some Merlin had touched them with his wand and bidden them drowse on for ever unchanged.

In the woods by the Hermit's pool this glamorous quiet is especially noticeable. Scarce a leaf stirs or a wavelet ripples; the air is warm and heavy with the dank colours of tree-bark, moss and waterweeds. Over the long vistas of the narrow pathways a light fleece of greyish-purple mist floats until midday, even when the sky above the tree-tops is gold-shot with sunshine and the heath outside crackling dry with heat. The beeches upon the shores of the lake are already in their full October glory of gold and russet and amber, every leaf and twig so faithfully reflected in the still waters that it seems that a second beechwood is submerged there, like one of the old drowned forests of legend.

Lately the solitude there has been invaded; a solitary angler has appeared, and stands, hunched like a human heron, fishing for hours from the farther bank. Although fish abound, I do not think he lands many; for yesterday, when he called at my cottage for a glass of water and presented me with a very small tench, that appeared to be the sole contents of his basket. As it was presented with the air of one presenting a lordly salmon, I could not refuse it without discourtesy; but after he had gone I stood for a long time looking at the torn mouth and spasmodically-convulsed form, and wondered how anyone could find pleasure in drawing a happy living thing from the cool, clear water to perish so miserably!. . .

Of all the trees of the wood the oak alone is untouched by the finger of autumn. "Laggard to come and laggard to go" is true of it in a seasonal sense as well as a lifelong. Not until really severe frost comes will the leaves blanch from their sober summer green, and even then they will hang and rustle upon the tree till the turn of the year comes and the sap rises.

The life-span of the oak is probably longer than that of any other living thing, animal or vegetable: "Three hundred years to come and grow. Three hundred to stand and stay. Three hundred to dwine and go", is the foresters' old adage about it. Even this may fall short; there are oaks still standing which are mentioned in the Doomsday Book, and they must have been well grown even then, or they would not have been selected for landmarks.

The fall of one of these giants of the woods is a moving sight. In the New Forest one day I happened to pass at the final crash of one. Woodmen stood around mopping their brows and congratulating each other upon the neat job they had made, guiding its fall scientifically to an inch to avoid injuring the branches of other trees.

"There it is, down in a day!" said one of them. "Down in a day! And not the wisest man in all the world could set it up again!"

But, noble as the New Forest oaks are, I have never, there or elsewhere, seen such a giant in girth as one I saw hauled through the streets of Oxford last month. Before it appeared the colleges, with their carved and crumbling antiquity, had seemed immemorial compared to the little span of man's mortality. Then through the narrow passage between them came the King of the Forest, its progress full of unpremeditated dignity, for its bulk was so great and the way so narrow that motor-buses, cars, cycles, and foot passengers had all to draw aside and wait while the traction-engine which drew it negotiated the turning.

Its length exceeded that of the timber-carriage upon which it was lashed, and it was supported at the end by a temporary extension. Its great grey girth, rough barked and fledged with lichens, brought the top of it on a level with balconies and upper windows. Its progress through the narrow streets had the slow stateliness of a procession.

To earn that pomp it had weathered who knows how many centuries? Standing, perhaps, upon some height above the city, it had looked down upon the Oxford of its saplinghood, a castle tower with a cluster of mud huts around; had watched spires and domes arise where before had been green meadows and glinting waterways, and seen those same spires and domes turn from snowy white to grey antiquity.

Of its thousand leafages some at least must have fluttered at the feet of men, then living in the flesh, whose names have also weathered the centuries. Shakespeare may have halted in its shade as he rode from Stratford to London, for it is a tradition that he always turned aside to sleep at the Davenant's hostelry. Shelley may have leaned against its trunk upon one of his country walks. Newman may have paced beneath, torn by inward questionings. Who can tell?

Now, after all the patient years, it had come down to the city, and bustling and impatient man stood aside to give it right of way. Perhaps one or two of those who stood at the crossing paid silent homage to its antiquity. All I heard was an American tourist complain to his daughter of the waste of time and protest against the way the traffic was controlled. A schoolboy brought forth his camera and snapped it. Motor-bus drivers chaffed the driver of the traction-engine: "Come along, old tortoise! Think we can wait all day for you to bring that old stump along?" and the old oak was coaxed round the corner, and the waiting crowd surged on.

But that progress through the street was the climax rather than the end. Timber of such soundness and proportions is of great value. A thing which neither science nor gold can hurry and only centuries of silent growth produce has, even in the market-place, a certain unique worth. As an oak screen, or beams, or perhaps as furniture the old oak has more centuries before it.

I sometimes reflect that it is one of the romances of common life that the wood used in our dwellings should once have been part of some living tree. The doors and window-frames of the most prosaic of suburban houses have probably waved, a tall pine, in some Scandinavian forest. The furniture has grown, an oak in an English hedgerow or a mahogany tree in a strange, far land.

One of my most cherished possessions is a table made from just such a tree as I saw in Oxford. The top of it is one wide plank polished like glass by the ministrations of generations of housewives; the legs are finely turned and carved and of a substance to defy time. I often look at it and wonder where and when it grew and wish it could tell of the summers and winters it knew and the generations which leaned against its trunk and rested in its shade...

Those who exclaim at the abundance of fungi in the woods in autumn might just as well exclaim at the scarcity, for if only one hundredth part of the spores of a single specimen survived, the earth the following year would be solid for yards with that particular kind. We all know the puff-ball of the pastures, and

how, when disturbed, a cloud of dark brown dust puffs from it; but not all of us have paused to consider that every microscopic speck of that dark brown dust is a living seed.

An interesting experiment may be made by taking a fully expanded common mushroom and placing it overnight, gills downward, upon a sheet of white paper. If the mushroom is lifted very carefully in the morning, the paper will be found to bear a delicately shaded replica of the under-side of the mushroom, every gill distinctly outlined in a soft brown. If this dark shading can be put under the microscope it will be found to consist of the thousands of infinitesimal spores, or seeds, which have fallen from the gills during the night.

The fungi of the woods are not confined to the surface mould. In the forks and upon the boughs of the oaks and beeches hang overlapping plates of a white substance, much like collections of oyster shells. This is the oyster mushroom, a popular dish amongst the greatly daring, who declare it tastes like a mixture of calves' liver and the best rump-steak. Brave spirits! I envy, but I dare not imitate, for I cannot forget that in the dictionary I use the word "Fungus" comes next to "Funeral"!

Upon the farther edge of the wood, enclosed in an angle of one of the ruined turf walls which are so common here, stand a yew and a spindle-wood tree. In mere years, no doubt, the spindle is a mere babe compared to the yew, but in appearance both are so hoary with age that they strike the observer as coeval survivors from some forgotten epoch.

The yew, at least, must be a thousand years old, for it is past its prime, and, although the lower boughs are red-rinded and dark-leaved, the upper trunk and branches stand stark against the sky. Against the dusty background of the yew the spindle tree is quite Japanese in its contortions; the boughs, with their twisted, grey-green bark, seem positively to writhe, and the leaves and berries are sprinkled so sparsely that they seem to decorate rather than clothe its antiquity.

A few feet from the earth the branches of the two trees mingle, and the flame-coloured leaves and pink and orange berries of the spindle-wood glow like clusters of some strange exotic flower against the drooping blackness of the yew. There is something strangely unfamiliar about these berries of the spindle-wood – berries which open out into dull pink segments, like petals, and expose a bright orange centre, which is really a seed.

Once, at an exhibition, I saw a dinner table decoration composed of them – sprays of bright leaves and drooping clusters of dull pink berries arranged in silver vases. On the orange silk table-centre below the vases more of the leaves were scattered, and the candle-shades repeated the dull pink of the berries.

A group of women were discussing the exhibit. One speaker thought the berries were some South African fruit, to which she gave a long native name. Another declared them "artificial", and not one seemed to recognise them as a product of our own English countryside.

Yet there was a time, not so many generations ago, when even a woman who knew nothing of trees in general, and cared less, being wholly taken up with her housekeeping, would have recognised the spindle-wood tree at a glance. In those days, when the spinning-wheel flashed beside every hearth, and everything possible was made at home, the tough, close-grained wood of the tree was in constant demand, and many a pair of lovers must have come to such a tree as this to choose a branch and cut it, to make a spindle for the lady's use.

Within the square of the turf wall, with the spindle and yew trees, stand two ancient apple trees, mossed up the trunks and bearded with lichen upon the branches, but still capable of a sprinkling of crinkled red and yellow pippins each year. Farther back in the square, half in the wood and half upon the heath outside, lie a few scattered blocks of the local brown ironstone: sure evidence that the turf wall once enclosed a cottage and garden, and that human beings were born, lived, loved and died where all is now given up to silence and solitude.

These low turf walls are a feature of the country round Peverel. Every-where, upon the Downs, in the woods, and even in the fields, they may be found, still enclosing spaces that were once homes, when all other vestiges of human occupancy have yielded to time. They are practically everlasting. A hundred years may sink them a few inches, a thousand years a few more inches; but, unless destroyed intentionally by man, they will still be distinct. Some of these walls show traces of a warlike purpose in the builders. Camps upon hill-crests are surrounded by them; in certain parts of the heath they run in parallel lines like trenches.

In the case of the enclosure in the wood, the fruit trees give a clue to a fairly recent occupancy; but after such evidences have perished it is impossible to tell the age of one. It may have been thrown up by the Celts or the Saxons, or by our own immediate ancestors a century or so ago. Very seldom, indeed, can the history of one be discovered, and the story of this one in the wood only came to me by accident; had I happened to have been walking elsewhere upon a particular morning last spring I should never have heard it.

I had come, then, to see the apple trees in flower, just as to-day I had gone for the spindle-berries. Upon the bank, in the deep shade, leaning back against the trunk of the yew, I found a very old man. In answer to my rather timid greeting, he pointed to the apple-blossom.

"Perhaps," he said, "you might not believe that my old great-granddad planted them trees."

I was not at all astonished: he looked old enough to have planted them himself. By simulating an appropriate expression of wonderment I became possessed of the whole history of the place.

About a hundred and fifty years ago my friend's ancestor, then "a spirity young chap" living in the New Forest, found that part of the country "too hot to hold him", on account of a slight misunderstanding about a deer found dead and half-skinned in his outhouse. Accompanied by his young wife, he fled from his native village and, avoiding keepers and verderers, made his way, chiefly by night, across country until he came to another land of forest and heath almost as wild as the one he had left.

For the first few months they lived in a sand-pit, striking across the heath, first to one village, then to another, for provisions. No one came near them; they were three miles from the nearest house, and cut off from it by both wood and water. When their money was spent the man found work upon a distant farm.

All day, while he was away, the wife collected lumps of sandstone from among the heather; at night the husband dug for more. When they had enough they started to build, rising at the first gleam of light in the morning, and continuing at night until darkness prevented them. For the rafters and window-frames they cut such timber as they could with the tools at their disposal, and thatched the whole with gorse from the heath.

Before the roof was on a son was born to them, an old Gipsy woman, who happened to be camping near, officiating as midwife. Before their presence was discovered by the authorities there were five children more; and, as by that time the seven years which gave them squatters' rights had expired, they were allowed to remain.

Time passed. The original Jack Stride died, and his son inherited. The generations came and went, each one adding something for comfort or ornament to the cottage, until, by the time my informant was a child, it was, as he said, "the neatest and tightest little place anywhere round about there", built in the shape of the letter L, and all smothered in jessamine and pink roses.

And the end of it? Well, it all came of quarrelling among brothers. When the last occupant died there was a large family left to inherit, and, while they disputed amongst themselves as to the division, the house meanwhile for some reason or other being unoccupied, the Lord of the Manor stepped in, claimed the ground, and had the cottage demolished.

"Just like a clutch of young birds squabbling in the nest, they were, and him like a girt old hawk a-swoopin' down upon 'em!" the old man concluded.

He had been but a small boy, the youngest of a large family, at the time; but somehow he was able to prove to his own satisfaction that the land where the cottage had stood was now his own individual property. For eighty years he had cherished the love of it and the ambition that one of his family might some day raise up another home there. His grandson, he said, was in Australia, doing well, and before he left he had said that, if ever he grew rich, he should return, buy the land, and build another house there.

Perhaps in the years to come he may; but the low brown cottage, shaped like an L, with jessamine and pink roses round the windows, has vanished like a dream. Not all the riches in the world can restore it . . .

The wind and rain at the end of last week began the first perceptible thinning of the woods. For a day and a night there was such a sobbing and sighing and gurgling of water everywhere that the very earth seemed to grieve for the passing of another season.

Along the woodland pathways, the leaves drifted in heavy wet masses of browns and crimsons and yellows. The last of the tall, bright garden flowers – hollyhocks, dahlias, and burning gladiolus spikes – were laid low in a tangled ruin on the wet soil. The rain swept in grey gusts across the stripped fields, and the sky hung leaden above the desolate earth.

There are a few days in the year when the weather makes the countryside really depressing. This was one of them, and long before the normal lighting-up time, the mind turned from the outer prospect to the cheerful fireside, drawn curtains, a book, and toast for tea.

This withdrawal from the outer world, pleasant enough in its way, proved premature. The next morning brought bright skies and air balmy as April, and country neighbours who the day before had prophesied the final breaking up of the season went to the other extreme and opined that, "with anything like luck, we med have six or eight weeks fine weather; an' nobody'd grumble if we had three months, for 't 'ud help th' Winter along finely; that's a fact it would".

Whether such good weather luck will come our way in England this Autumn is doubtful, but the few days of sunshine we have had, taken alone, are something to thank St Martin for.

This respite before Winter, known in different countries as St Martin's Summer, the Indian Summer, the Little Summer of All Saints, and by other beautiful and endearing names, is one of the most fascinating features of our climate. I do not think any other country has anything like it. It is quite different from the clear, crisp Autumn weather of a week or two back, and still more unlike the still, grey days ahead of us. Excepting for the brilliant earth-tints which the rain has freshened, these mild, sunny, misty days are more like the first warm days of early Spring than any other time of year. There are the same soft airs and the same fleecy clouds and the same earthy odours of turf and moss as there were at the end of March . . .

At one time it was believed that the swallow hibernated in the same way as the bat is known to do. The idea arose, no doubt, through the habit these birds have of congregating in large flocks a few miles inland from the Channel coast in Autumn and disappearing and re-appearing at intervals of a few days for several weeks. The patient observations of bird-lovers during the last hundred and twenty years have established the knowledge that these congregations are composed of different birds, one flock departing overseas and another from farther north taking its place; but a century ago this disappearance and re-appearance had not been accounted for, and it was thought that in bad weather the swallows retired to some winter retreat close at hand, to be coaxed out again by every spell of fine weather until the Winter finally closed down. Then, as they were so often to be seen skimming the surface of the water at that time, it followed that they should be supposed to hibernate either in the crevices of the banks of ponds and streams, or to plunge, fishlike, into the warm mud at the bottom.

That most famous of our early birdlovers, Gilbert White, of Selborne, played with this idea all his life. Although he was convinced that the majority of the swallow families migrated, he thought it just possible that the weaker birds of the late broods might remain in this country, and, in order to settle the question, he offered a handsome reward to anyone who could produce a hibernating swallow for his inspection. Naturally enough, although there were country people who were ready to swear they had seen the birds hanging from the rafters like bats, or had helped to fish them in masses from the bottom of ponds, not a single specimen was forthcoming.

That every schoolboy is better informed as to the habits of birds in these days than the greatest living naturalist was then we owe to the tireless zeal and humble seeking for truth of such men as Gilbert White and his circle of correspondents . . .

To-day the squirrels have been almost frantic over the last scramble to collect yet one more hoard of nuts to store, and the wood has been full of the small sounds of their activity as they chased each other at full speed from tree-top to tree-top, or pattered among the dry leaves beneath the hazel bushes.

Each squirrel family makes a number of such collections, burying them in the soft leaf-mould among the mosses, or packing them away into tree-hollows or beneath roots – little larders, all ready in case their owners should wake and feel hungry at midwinter.

The squirrel is a light sleeper, and a day or two of mild winter sunshine will always bring it out; but the nuts and acorns collected are almost always more than it requires, and many of the hoards are left underground to germinate and spring up to make the forests of the future.

The hedgehog needs no such storehouses. At the first sharp frost it will roll itself into a prickly ball, thrust itself into some slight depression among the dead leaves, and remain dead to the world, come sunshine, come snow, until the primroses are out.

The hibernation of the dormouse is even more complete. Cold and rigid to the touch, its little flame of life turned down to the merest spark, it sleeps so profoundly that its small body is often taken for a corpse.

Certain reptiles simulate death even more effectually. We have all heard the story of the absurdly kind-hearted woodman who warmed the frozen snake in his bosom; also of the old woman who picked up an adder in mistake for a stick and carried it home in her faggot, and, if either tale has a foundation of truth, both reptiles were probably hibernating.

Our native snakes do not, as a rule, expose themselves to the risk of such mistaken kindness. By mid-October they vanish from the earth as completely as though they had never been, to lie tucked away with slow-worms, lizards, and toads in chinks in rough stone walls or quarry faces, or beneath isolated rocks upon the moors.

Even the frog turns its back upon winter weather and forces its way through the smallest possible opening into cavities so tiny that its soft, squat body fits into them like a jelly in a mould. Sometimes during the winter, the rock or stones about it will slide, cover the opening chink, and leave poor Froggie a prisoner. Captured thus, the frog has the strange power of supporting life for months, or even years, without food, or with only such food as can be obtained by darting its long tongue for flies through some microscopic opening . . .

It is a pity so many of the old field-names are becoming obsolete. Fifty, thirty, even twenty years ago, every field had its own immemorial name, just as it still keeps its own individuality, no two fields anywhere being exactly alike in shape, size, and soil. A field now is too often but a field, the farms pass from owner to owner, from tenant to tenant; the sons of the old labouring families migrate to towns, disillusioned townsmen take their places, and the old names are allowed to lapse.

Some of these names explained themselves. "Charlcroft's" was an echo of the reign of a once important local family. "Lark's Lease" – poor in soil and rich in skylark's song, though at least two centuries had passed since it was named on that account.* Loam Pits, Pond Piece, Sanfoin, and Forty Acres were plain, straightforward names. But what could be made of Duffus Piece?

That last name used to puzzle me. Was Duffus, I wondered, a former owner, or should it really be Duffer's, in memory of some forgotten boggling of its crop one year? It interested me particularly at the time because, staying in a midland village, I had chosen that one rich, tree-shaded meadow in a broad expanse of arable land to rest and read in through the midsummer heat.

Another puzzling feature of the field was that, strewn beneath bushes and among the coarse grass, in one corner were a number of large stone-blocks. Evidently there had once been a building of some sort, although no trace of the foundations remained. It must have been a structure of some importance too, for the ashlars were well squared, and many of them pierced with an opening like a tiny doorway. Whatever purpose they had served had been long forgotten. They may have lain there for centuries, cut off as they were from the rest of the meadow by a trickle of muddy water known locally as the Moat.

Beyond the meadow and the trickling water was a dense tangle of shrubbery which hedged in the grounds of an ancient Manor House. Scarcely anything was known in the village of this house or its occupants. Generations had passed since the last "Squire", then a young man newly married, had tripped over his

---

*These field names are clearly local to Juniper Hill, since the author was "staying in a midland village at the time". Duffus Piece and Pond Piece are mentioned in *Lark Rise,* chapter III.

spur running downstairs on a hunting morning, and his widow, now an old lady of over ninety, had never since been known to leave the grounds.

She lived so absolutely alone that the finely-wrought iron entrance gates had rusted upon their hinges, and what had been the front drive was completely choked with shrubs and tree-boughs. But even grief and eccentricity cannot live wholly without contact with the outer world, and the back premises were open to tradesmen and villagers who came with jugs· to buy pennyworths of skim milk.

My opportunity to see within came with a milk shortage. My landlady was old and inactive, and what more natural than that I should offer to run up to the House for a jugful?

I entered a flagged courtyard, a little awed by the intense silence. Weeds grew up between the stones, and, even in the full afternoon light, birds whirred out in flocks from the ivy about the iron-clamped door. Afterwards I learned that I should have taken another path to a humbler entrance, that this was the "old part", where no villager was allowed to go. The sound of the heavy lion-head knocker reverberated from one empty room to another, but no one came to dispel the air of romantic uncanniness, and I felt as though I had strayed by accident into some medieval fairy-tale.

All about me was crumbling stone. The surrounding walls were falling into grit and eaten into by yellow lichen. Ferns and wallflowers sprang from the crevices, and every ledge was topped by house-leek and valerian. Near the door stood a long stone drinking trough, coffin-shaped; it may have served as a human coffin at some time or other – probably had. In the centre of the court was a stone well-head, from which the woodwork had long since crumbled.

But what interested me most was the top of a strange circular building which rose above the courtyard wall. It was the size of a small cottage, round in shape as a Laplander's hut, and open to the sky, excepting for a skeleton dome of heavy stonework. Most puzzling feature of all, the walls were pierced all over with the little doorways like desk pigeon-holes I had noticed in the scattered stones in the field.

As, despairing of an answer, I turned at last to go, I found a little old woman at my elbow. She was so old and bent and so very shabbily dressed that I might have taken her for a beggar had she not raised her hand with an imperious gesture, as though to rebuke my temerity in waking the echoes.

"The dairy," she said, with a disdainful glance at my jug, "is round the corner by the Duffus."

"I am sorry-" I began, but she cut my apology short.

"Round by the Duffus," she repeated, and waved a chalk-white hand in the direction of the curious circular building. "The Duffus – the *dove-house* – the *pigeon-house!* You will find a path there, which you will kindly keep to in future. I allow no trespassers here."

So, through this queer little adventure, I found the clue to the field-name. A dove-house had once stood there, an institution contemporary with unglazed windows and rushes strewn on floors for a carpet. Centuries must have passed since that particular dove-house had been populous with white wings, and centuries before that had seen it as much a part of the economy of the house as the fish-pond, or as the kitchen-garden is now; but the field was still Duffus or Dove-house Piece – the name the only clue to its history . . .

In bird life the last few weeks has seen many changes. Only a fortnight ago the swallows and house-martins were still with us, stringing themselves along the telephone wires, haunting the pools, and hawking for insects between the hills, so much a part of the scenery that it was difficult to imagine the place without them.

Then came a night of frost, followed by a day of cold winds, and, when the sky was clear again, the swallows had vanished. Long before they were missed, no doubt, they had left England far behind, for the swallow birds are strong and swift on the wing, and, granted favouring winds, think nothing of breakfasting in Sussex and supping on the shores of the Meditteranean. Now they are still further south, and the same bird which built under our cottage eaves may at this moment be circling a pyramid or sipping at the margin of one of the great hidden African lakes.

Very few observers have ever witnessed the actual migration. Lighthouse keepers in time of storm or fog have reported the enforced landing of a flock upon their buildings or rocks, and now and then, under similar circumstances, they have been known to descend to the decks and rigging of ships at sea; but such sights are unusual. In normal migrating weather they fly so high in the air that their forms can only be discerned with the aid of a powerful telescope.

More wonderful still than the flight of those strong voyagers of the upper air is the annual migration of so many of the warbler tribe. Willow-wren, blackcap, wood-wren and chiff-chaff – no one remarked their going, but they have gone, and it is quite certain that the seemingly weak little wings that seemed to halt even in their flitting from bush to bush, have borne their tiny owners across oceans and continents.

Other migrants have arrived here from the north. In and out of the alder boughs which overhang the stream a bevy of siskins flit and twitter. Their actions as they hop from twig to twig are very like those of caged canaries; and canary-like, too, the gold and fawn and yellowish green of their plumage. It is a pretty sight to see them hang, head downwards, to investigate the inside of the seed-vessels of the alder in search of the food they love. All day they remain in the one row of trees, flirting their bright wings and uttering their sweet, soft-twittering note, something like that of the linnet, but clearer and stronger.

Sometimes during the winter they disappear for weeks, probably crossing the Channel to lands still further south, reappearing for a few days in the early spring on their way back to their homes in the fir forests of Norway or Sweden.

A complete contrast to their sweet, plaintive note is the hoarse "Chack! Chack!" which greets us in the fields these autumn days. That sure herald of winter, the fieldfare, is with us once more. If it were ever seen singly this bird might easily be mistaken for our own misselthrush, for, though somewhat smaller in build, colouring and marking are very similar, the chief distinction

being that, while the misselthrush keeps to its warm brown and fawn tints throughout, the back of the fieldfare has a dark bluish tinge.

But, though resembling each other in looks, the habits of the two birds are quite different, for, while the misselthrush is essentially a solitary tree-loving bird, the fieldfare spends its time with us wheeling in large flocks about the fields, crowding to moist and marshy spots for worms; or, taking to the heath, the whole flock will settle as one upon a thorn, to strip it of its whole crop of haws at a meal.

In its native Norway, they say, the fieldfare has a sweet, wild song which is much beloved; but it is one of those rare singers who keep their best music for home, and all we hear of it during its winter sojourn is the loud, grating call-note which, blending with the melancholy call of the pee-wit, makes the cold wind seem colder and the waste spaces more desolate.

As these wild invaders settle in the fields our own native songsters draw nearer to the habitations of man. Blackbird and song-thrush establish their claim to the shrubberies about the house; the bluetits return to the garden to search the exact spot where last year's cocoanut was suspended for their benefit; linnet and skylark echo each other beyond the gate and the yellow-hammer haunts the hedge with his exasperated request for "a little bit of bread and *no* cheese!"

Sweetest and most characteristic of all autumn songs is that of the Robin Redbreast. All day long he follows the gardener around, so much at home that he will perch himself upon the very spade-handle if it is left idle a while, taking toll of the worms and grubs from the freshly-turned earth, or, upon the topmost twig of a nearby bush, giving thanks for his meal with a burst of song, silvery sweet and clear.

Nor, much as he makes himself at home there, does he keep wholly to the garden. Robin is everywhere at this time of year – in the woods, by the hedgerows, and even out among the hollies upon the heath. At every turn his red breast may be sighted, like an animated autumn leaf, as he flutters from bush to bush, always a few yards in advance of the wayfarer whose walk he is apparently sharing.

His is the first song in the morning and the last at night in these autumn days, frequently ringing out after dusk has fallen, and bearing in such surroundings a quite presentable resemblance to that of his noble relative, the nightingale.

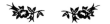

November

November

*T*HE GORSE IS a curious instance of the strange power plants as well as animals have of adapting themselves to circumstances. Mark the rudimentary leaf – a mere spine. What could be more appropriate to a plant which has to wrest a living from the hungry soil of the dry uplands, where leaf-surface is a luxury, meaning, as it does, a myriad of small mouth-like pores, each one demanding moisture and nourishment? Yet, sow a seed or two of the gorse in a flower-pot indoors, and in a week or two you will see soft little trefoils of green appear, more like the leaf of the clover or laburnum than the prickly spine you expected.

Such, botanists tell us, was the original form of the gorse leaf; but gradually, to survive at all, it had to cut down its demands to meet its resources, and, as a reward for its frugality, it flourishes in places where most other plants would starve. Yet, hardy as it appears, it is not as widely distributed as might be expected; it does not grow farther north than Scotland, and in Russia is cultivated as a hot-house plant. It cannot grow wild in Sweden either, for we are told that when Linnaeus, the great botanist, came to England he threw himself upon his knees and thanked the Creator for permitting him to live to see the golden glory of an English common with the gorse in bloom.

Alas! in nature, as in art, we gain only according to our capacity. You cannot put an ocean into a pint pot; and so, too, many of us pass daily such sights as that which stirred Linnaeus, and notice only the prickles catching at our clothes.

Beyond the gorse, at the top of a little pine-crowned hillock, a small mound of twigs and pine-needles, in size and shape much like a beach-playing child's sandcastle, has been accumulating all the summer. I had noticed it vaguely as I passed to the pool each day, but had not troubled to investigate until the other day, when, as I was filling my basket with fir-cones, I happened to stir the apex, and found it was more of a city than a castle into which I had broken.

It was the work of the red wood ants, a marvel of construction. Small compartments, connected by corridors, were arranged story above story to a number rivalling an American sky-scraper. Although the roof and part of the side of their home had gone at one sweep, the inmates showed no panic, but thronged the corridors in ordered files like marching soldiers in their dull rust-red uniforms.

These red wood ants, or horse ants, as they are sometimes called, are the largest, and throw up the most conspicuous mounds of our British species; but the commoner variety, found with their mounds of earth in pastures, upon roadsides, or any waste places, are equally interesting to watch.

"Go to the ant," said the wise man long ago; "study her ways, and be wise." Countless generations of men and insects have flourished and passed away since he said it, but the good example of the ant is just as well worth following to-day as it was then. The ant was probably the first co-operator. "Each for all and all for each" has always been its motto. It forms communities in which all the inhabitants work cheerfully for the common weal; each individual has its definite place in the scheme of things, and its appointed task to perform. Amongst those I saw to-day, two upon the outskirts of the mound were hauling a pine-twig between them; almost beyond their strength it seemed, for it was in bulk equal to at least ten of its bearers, but they pushed and pulled at it, stopping every few seconds to rest, until they were within a few inches of their goal. Then a surprising thing happened. From the citadel came a relief party. Four found easy the task which had overtaxed two. The rest of the journey was made without a halt, and the twig was soon in its appointed place.

But, although the ant is such a hard worker, it has its playtime, too. The microscope will show them skipping about upon their hind legs and embracing each other with their antennae in a kind of dance. They have their domestic animals, too. The green aphides one finds upon rose-trees are kept and milked by them, just as man keeps cows.

In one respect they lag behind civilized man, for one at least of our native species are slave-owners. The next time you come across an ant-heap examine it, and, if you find it tenanted by two different species together, be sure that the larger insect is the master, the smaller the slave. These small jet-black slave-ants are carried off from their home nest in the pupa stage and trained to perform the manual work of the large red-headed, red-thighed ant, their captor.

One very touching incident in ant-life takes place when the female, back from her marriage flight, prepares to make a home for the coming generation. The first thing she does is to nip off her own wings lest she should be tempted to disport herself in the sunshine, to the detriment of her maternal duties. There is something very human about this action, as many of my readers who are mothers will understand. I wonder no modern novelist has taken it for a text . . .

And so one finds, when we come to study a small stretch of country at all intensively, that every field and lane, every tree and clod, has a history. I wonder that no educationist has suggested that the school children of a parish should be appointed its historians. What a multitude of interesting, yet little regarded, facts, likely to be intensely interesting to future generations, those small, sharp eyes would note.

In this parish, for instance, the shell of a hollow tree was recently felled to make way for the builder. Up to just before the war there was still a floating legend that this tree, two miles distant from the present forest bounds, had once marked the verge of the Royal Forest of Woolmer. It was swept away unnoted. Not even a paragraph in the local paper recorded the going of it.

If the school history had been in being, the disappearance of so ancient a landmark would certainly have been chronicled, with a description of the exact spot where it stood, and perhaps a snapshot to show to what a mere hollow tooth of a tree it had dwindled.

Supposing the school history had been in being before Queen Anne put the pinnacle upon her renown by dying, upon the day the old tree fell we should have turned back the pages for the description by an eye-witness of the procession of that Queen and her courtiers beneath the green and spreading boughs of that same tree in its prime. That she did pass beneath it as she went to review her drove of red deer in Woolmer we know; but, having no child-historian to appeal to, only the bare fact of her passing that way is thrown to us incidentally.*

And not less interesting would it be centuries hence to those for whom the great war would be but "an old, unhappy, far-off thing, a battle long ago", to

---

*See page 175 above.

learn from the school history that the soldiers in those old romantic times camped upon such a heath, or drilled in such a field.

Then our history, linking all the country together in a network of parishes, would be a natural history, too. Records would be kept of climatic conditions, of rare bird visitors, of the making or draining of ponds, of the planting and felling of woods, and so on.

The connection of any famous, or likely to become famous name with the place would be found there, too. The well-known poet who stayed at the hotel, and spent hours gazing upon a certain view; the farmer's son, a native born, who became an engineer and patented a world-shaking invention – such facts as could be obtained without impertinence relating to such ones would be there, ready to the hand of future biographers.

It would make interesting reading for the people of the year 2,000, this "New Domesday Book; or Every Parish its Own Historian"!...

Against the sky in the bare thorns the nests of last spring are exposed: some of them so placed that it seems impossible they could ever have been hidden. Those in the outer forks near the path must have been set swinging a hundred times by the brushing shoulder of the passer-by. Now that the leaves are gone is the time to study the construction of the different nests – the hedge-sparrow's loose bundle of coarse grass; the blackbird's and thrush's mudcup; the wren's compact ball of moss and dry leaves, and the wonderfully woven moss, wool, and feathers of the chaffinch's nest.

In examining them we are bound to come across those pretty red and green moss-balls upon the wild-rose briar that children call "bird's-nests" or Robin's Pincushions. A spray holding one of them is an effective addition to our nose-gay; but, pretty as they are, these mossy balls are neither flower nor fruit, but partly animal and partly vegetable in origin. Months ago, a tiny gall-fly

crawled up the branch where the Robin's Pincushion now appears to pierce the rind and lay its eggs beneath, and when the grubs were hatched out the acid fluid thrown off by them caused structural changes in the vegetable cells, which resulted in the pretty flower-like ball of green and red.

Other trees have different gall-fly guests. The one frequenting the oak is responsible for the oak-apple; that visiting the sycamore for the little waxen-red spangles upon the underside of the leaves. These spangles may also be found upon the leaves of the briar, and it is no uncommon thing to find that two different species of gall-fly have visited the same bough.

Another sign of a visiting insect may be seen just now upon the bramble. Upon many of the deep crimson leaves may be found pale wavy markings, much like handwriting, into which fancy may read mystic characters of unknown import. These markings are due to the appetite of the larvae of a tiny two-winged fly called the "diptera", which eats its way in a kind of tunnel through the fleshy side of the leaf, leaving the fibrous matter intact. When the colour deepens in the normal cells the destroyed part shows up, a pale straw-colour against the bronze or crimson . . .

In the woods, the upper boughs stand clear and leafless, but from the lower and inner branches the leaves still float in sufficient numbers for those who believe in the old superstition that for every leaf caught in the hand between tree and earth one year of happiness is assured, to register a lifetime without trouble. Around the boles the bracken is still yellow, and the heather in sheltered nooks retains a faint blush of pale purple.

While these late lingerers fade gradually, the mosses and lichens are brightening to another blooming. In the woods in winter they may be seen in their full beauty, thriving upon damp and cold as other plants do upon sunshine: the mosses rising, golden-green, feathery or clubbed, from dead leaves and withered herbage; the lichens splashing the rugged bark of trees with orange, rust, and smoke-grey, hanging from the leafless thorns like beards, and covering flat stones and naked earth with patterns embossed in black or yellow.

Strange plants! The winter of all other vegetation is their spring; and at the dead of the year, just before and after Christmas, many a bank and hillside will be brightened with their flowering. At that season a small microscope adds greatly to the pleasure of country ramblers. By its aid a thousand unsuspected beauties are revealed; splashes of rust or orange are seen as whole flower gardens within a few square inches, and the sight of the infinitesimal cup or star-shaped florets is bound to lead to the study of the structure and habits of the different varieties.

But the interest the mosses and lichens possess for us does not end with their marvellous structure and beauty; they have a long history behind them – the longest of anything living. They are the oldest inhabitants of this earth of ours. In our own country, it is said, they appeared as early as the glacial period, long before there was animal or other vegetable life. First came the lichens, attaching themselves to the bare rocks and drawing their sustenance from the atmosphere, generation after generation of them, thriving, decaying, and leaving behind its tiny residue of soil until there was sufficient for the mosses to appear and continue the work. Without their lowly labour there could have been no rose, no lily, no wheat or forest tree, for, before a leaf or blade could appear, the lichens and mosses had to prepare soil for them to root in.

These two plants in their different varieties are still the most widely spread of all vegetable life. From the tropics to the Arctic circle, in jungle swamps and above the snow-line of mountains, they may be found, little labourers, as a great botanist once lovingly called them, humbly performing their part in the great scheme of nature.

At one time various mosses and lichens were used extensively both as food and in medicine. One species of lichen called rock-tripe is still a favourite dish in Iceland, and herbalists in our own country still use one of our native kinds as an emollient for chest complaints. During the war, too, on account of its softness and antiseptic qualities, the sphagnum moss was found useful for dressing wounds, and many of my readers will, no doubt, remember the long hours spent picking the dry fragments of leaves and twigs from it. The same moss grows in Lapland, where mothers use it to line the cradles of their new-born babes. To the sphagnum, too, we owe our deliciously-smelling peat fires in winter, for the pear is chiefly composed of countless generations of sphagnum and other mosses which have decayed, soaked in bog-water, undergone certain chemical changes, and dried into the solid layer which is cut into blocks for burning.

Against the green of the mosses in the woods this month the late autumn fungi stand in all manner of fantastic shapes, some brightly coloured, others ivory white, spongy yellow, or ranging through all the dingy browns of decay. Beneath the pine trees the ruddy warty-cap still flourishes like flowers in a garden, its glowing brick-coloured disc set off with yellow bosses. For those adventurous ones who dare to eat fungi, this favourite dish of theirs is still in season, but most of the other edible kinds have fallen into most unappetising decay. The bolet, or penny bun, no longer looks freshly glazed from the baker's oven, as it did a few weeks ago, but has swollen into monstrous shapes, great sponges and umbrellas turned inside out, masses of corruption, over which slugs crawl and bluebottles hover.

Upon one huge specimen I overturned to-day an assembly of tiny white snails had gathered, whether for food or warmth I cannot say. This little white snail, "pulchella", as it is called by the scientific observer, is very common upon the South Downs. Being only about the tenth of an inch in circumference, it is often taken for the baby of the yellow Roman snail, but it is a quite distinct family, and the tiny, bead-like atoms are already fully grown. Upon the Downs it may be seen in scores, clustering upon the wild thyme and other short herbage; and it is said to contribute largely to the richness and flavour of the famous Southdown mutton.

The snails alone would make a winter walk in the most commonplace scenery interesting, for it is surprising to find the number of varieties existing side by side in any lane or hedgerow. The spotted or garden snail is a common sight everywhere, although few notice it, excepting children and gardeners. Between the snail and the latter there is a deadly feud (deadly to the snail, at least), for its taste in vegetables is too human to make it a welcome guest in any garden. The youngest of green peas, the crispest of lettuce, the fattest asparagus stems, the peach ripening upon the wall – the taste for such things is fitting in man, but out of place in a snail.

Children and boys are the only friends of the garden snail; the former love to hold it by the shell and chant the immemorial charm:

> "Snail, snail, put out your horn,
> And then I'll give you a barleycorn,"

just for the pleasure of seeing the sensitive horns, in which, most probably, the snail's senses of sight, touch, and hearing are concentrated, slowly and cautiously put out, as though newly growing.

These largest of our land snails were a favourite dish with the Romans in Britain, and are said to be eaten in certain districts in the West of England to this day. If so, the cooks in those parts deserve credit, for once during the war, inspired by a newspaper article, I experimented upon a dish of them. After an elaborate and prolonged preparation my dish was set upon the table, in appearance much like stewed oysters in melted butter. Alas for appearances! The should-have-been savoury tit-bits tasted exactly like morsels of stewed rubber; and, although I brought both the appetite and the obstinacy of the pioneer to the dish, I could not away with even one of its contents.

In spite of this personal failure, it is quite probable that no one need starve while there are slugs and snails to be found and a fire is forthcoming to cook them by. In a certain village in the Midlands there used to be a tradition dating from the old sheep-stealing days that once a poor widow with a large family was suspected of receiving and hiding stolen mutton, because, having no means excepting the starvation allowance of the relieving officer, her children were yet the plumpest and rosiest in the parish. One day the authorities searched her cottage and found a barrel of meaty morsels salted down in her larder. This at first was taken for finely minced mutton, but, upon examination, proved to be slugs which she gathered in wet weather to provide all the meat her children were likely to taste . . .

The men employed upon the tree-felling have built themselves a shelter of boughs in the clearing, where the camp fire, with its tripod suspended kettle, gives a pleasant, homely touch to the whole proceeding. The men shout directions to each other and sing as they work. All day the sound of the axe rings out through the woods, and presently comes the tragic rending and tearing of centuries of growth, followed by the final crash.

It is a sad but necessary business, for the trees have long passed their prime, and in a few years would but cumber the ground. As it is, the wood is too full of flaws for any purpose but fire-logs. To the experienced woodman, the sight of an old oak with dead branches at its crown, "dying upon its legs" as they call it, is an abomination.

Such men, to do them justice, are just as proud of any remarkably ancient or historically interesting specimen under their care as others, and never at a loss to find means to preserve it; but the sight of the merely decrepit fills them with rage, for such lingerers not only crumble to waste themselves, but occupy space which ought to be planted for posterity.

No generation of men can plant oaks for its own benefit. Those trees which are being felled and used to-day were planted in a world without railway trains, and those now being planted will lend beauty and give service to an age in which wireless telegraphy may quite probably be superseded.

Then, again, to preserve a tree beyond its prime is a form of waste. Even one fine oak may be sold for a large enough sum to plant a considerable wood. Just before the war, for instance, some very choice oaks, with timber of the dark brown shade so much in demand for cabinetmaking, were sold for one hundred pounds each as they stood, the purchaser taking the risk of unsuspected flaws.

Ordinary specimens do not, of course, fetch so much; but every sound oak has its value as timber, and to realise this at the moment its beauty begins to decline is part of the art of good forestry.

The planting of young trees is not only an art, but a duty, which conscientious estate owners take seriously. Some there are, it is true, who are known to boast that they never fell an old tree; but as these sentimentalists are often the very men who neglect planting, they are as bad in their way as the vandal who turns all the timber on his estate into ready money.

Very different was the temper of that old country squire who, stricken with mortal disease, found his one remaining pleasure in strolling round his estate with a spud in his hand and a pocket full of acorns. That was the action of an earth-lover who had no time to lose.

Usually saplings are planted which have been raised from seed in the tree-nursery attached to every estate which has extensive woodlands. Other rarer kinds are imported, and laurels, rhododendrons and other shrubs planted as undergrowth; so that very often the wood which appears to the inexperienced eye as an example of Nature's wildest luxuriance owes at least something to human taste.

Disturbed by the fall of some hollow tree, where they had hung themselves up to sleep, a number of bats had faced the daylight this morning and flittered about the clearing where the men were at work. Perhaps they were deceived by the dim light into thinking it late afternoon, for these were the pipistrelles, or flittermice, the smallest and commonest of all our twelve native bats, and they will sometimes fly quite early in the evening.

Seen thus in the twilight, the flittermouse at first sight is often taken for a bird, but very soon, as it flits to and fro, its sudden abrupt dartings and turnings proclaim its true nature. The small, shrill squeak it utters as it flies is rather more mouse-like than bird-like, but actually it resembles no other sound in nature, being so thin and high that it eludes the hearing of many people, and is far more like the sharp, sudden scratch of a pencil upon a slate than the voice of a living creature.

The bat is an example of a dog with a bad name. Although perfectly innocent, it is regarded by many with the same unreasoning horror as the toad or the slow worm. Painters have used its quaint form as a symbol to surround allegorical figures of darkness and evil. Country people used to believe it had a vampire-like tendency to blood-sucking, and some portion of a bat's anatomy figured in the recipe for every witches' brew or hate potion.

But, stripped of such outworn associations, the bat has a quaint charm of its own, being a soft dark-grey furred, mouse-like little creature, with a sharp, foxlike face and upstanding ears.

The wing structure of the bat is unique, the first joint of the forelegs being elongated and joined to the sides by the thick leathery membrane which forms the "wing". Upon the ground its superficial resemblance to a bird disappears, and it scrambles on all fours, the grace of its progress ruined by the now useless wings, which do not, however, appear to impede it, for it travels at quite a respectable rate. Witnesses say that should a bat find itself accidentally plunged into water, it uses its wings as oars and rows quickly to land.

Next to the little flittermouse, or pipistrelle, the great bat is the most commonly seen of our native species. This flies higher and is stronger and straighter in flight than the flittermouse, and, while the latter includes every kind of night-flying insect in its diet, the former lives chiefly upon the larger beetles, especially the cockchafer.

All bats are nocturnal in their habits. All day they hide away in church towers, hollow trees, in railway tunnels, amongst the rafters of barns and lofts, or in any other dark and fairly inaccessible nook. There, in the darkness, they suspend themselves by the claws, heads downward and wings folded – seldom singly, but in bunches of from two or three to a dozen or more.

The breeding habits of bats are very curious. Although the parents mate in autumn, the young are not born until the following spring, when they come into the world blind, bare and helpless. As a general rule, only one is produced at a birth, and this the mother carries with her wherever she goes, the little one clinging with its claws to the maternal fur, so that often the supposed vampire and creature of ill omen we see flitting about us in our twilight walks is really a good, domesticated little mother taking her baby for an airing.

In another wood near here they are cleaning a pond – a deep, circular, tree-shaded pool, with steep banks eaten into caves by the lapping of the water – and during the draining process a number of large pike were stranded, while others saved their lives by burrowing into the mud at the bottom of the small pools left by the irregularities of the pond-bed.

This pond, as one of the men employed upon the cleaning remarked, is "just about a top-notch Pikes' Paradise", for there is nothing that a fish loves so well as a muddy pool, where it can lurk unsuspected among the weeds or hide in a cavity in one of the banks, ready to dart out its cruel, shark-like head and snap up its prey as it swims past.

Frogs, fish, young ducklings, frog-spawn and grubs and insects of all kinds – nothing that is to be found in or about the water comes amiss to its voracious appetite. It will swallow another pike as readily as any other fish; and even as to size it is not at all discriminating, many a large old pike having perished in the attempt to put one of its still larger brethren away. No wonder that in ponds where they live undisturbed these cannibals grow to an immense size, eight, ten, or even a dozen pounds being common, while many have been caught which turned the scale at over twenty.

Now a few, at least, of the monsters have gone to their reckoning, for during the last few days the stranded fish have been carried in buckets and sacks to the neighbouring hamlet to make meals not only for the workmen and their families, but for neighbours as well.

As an incentive to generosity, the pike comes next to the vegetable marrow, both on account of its size and because, no matter how daintily it is served – stuffed with forcemeat and baked, plainly boiled with melted but-

ter, or fried to a glorious golden-brown, its flesh is so extremely satisfying that nobody wants a second helping, while a second dish within a week is unthinkable.

So for one evening there was much running to and fro and a great sizzling of frying-pans, and the savoury odours of cooking mingled with the scent of wood smoke and the mist of November woods . . .

It is the fashion to talk of our changing climate and bewail the hot summers and hard winters of tradition, but how seldom we pause to marvel at the remarkable constancy of the weather from year to year.

No matter how mild and open the winter, we may count upon a cold snap at the end of January; while the first week in February more often than not brings a premature foretaste of spring. April, again, is sure to bring a mixture of all the months, and August would not be August without thunder rumbling around.

Our Saxon forefathers called November "Wintmonath", or Wind Month, and still, after a thousand years, the November gales return.

All last night, a strong north-easter swept over the Downs, ruffling the bracken, bending the pines, and lashing each small, tranquil pond into a miniature ocean. It rushed through the valley, and the straw-ricks, left unthatched from yesterday's thrashing, were whirled in the air and away.

In the woods the acorns hurtled through the darkness like duck-shot. The great beeches screeched like seaside shingle in a tempest; the oaks roared bull-like, while the hollies beat their polished leaves together, like a million applauding hands. Just before dawn the wind sank into little sobbing gusts, and day broke, grey, wet and unpromising.

A changed world, indeed, the raw daylight revealed. Autumn had lowered her flag at last, and all her bright colours were huddled out of sight. Where yesterday the last fires of the beech woods smouldered, bare boughs stood gaunt against a dull grey sky. The wet earth was dark; the water steely, and over all was the dripping sky we have most of us grown so heartily tired of.

The outer world looked so dismal, the indoor room, with its books and firelight and flowers, so tempting, that it seemed almost perverse to go out. But, reflecting that all through the wet summer the day I had arranged to collect these notes upon had each month happened to be fine, I took down my raincoat and buckled on my stoutest brogues . . .

A small local curiosity in these parts this year is a black and white-streaked blackbird – a quaint, unnatural look-ing creature, with its magpie marking and shape and motions of its own kind. Although I had never seen one before, I believe such freaks of bird-life are not uncommon, both white-and-black and pure white blackbirds being reported from time to time in the newspapers.

Scientific observers tell us that these variations are due to a form of *albinism*; but it would be more poetic to imagine them an attempt on the part of the individual bird to revert to the primitive whiteness of its race. For the blackbird, so the legend goes, was white as the driven snow until it attempted to rob a certain ogre of his hoard of fairy gold. Then the flames which burst forth from the threatened treasure so singed and blackened its plumage that ever since it has been black from tip to tail. Only its bill, permanently gilded from contact with so much bright gold, has for ever retained its brightness.

December

December

SO QUIET AND subtle is the beauty of December that it escapes the notice of many people their whole lives through. To them it is simply a winter month to be lived through somehow; they bracket it with January and November as "the dead of the year".

Yet it has its own characteristic beauty. It is, of all the year, the time when colour gives place to form; the trees, stripped of their autumn brilliance, stand, every branch and twig distinct, in a delicate dark tracery against the sky; the downs, now that the heath and bracken are beaten down, stand firmer and sharper of outline; new vistas, obscured all the summer by leafage, open up between them. The earth renews herself, not in spring only, but at every season.

Then, again, on December days of sun and wind, what a pageantry of cloud scenery we have; no other month, unless it be March, can match it. Clouds piled in Alps upon the horizon; clouds in fleets, scudding before the wind across an azure sea of sky; clouds in fleeces, white or yellow or rainbow touched like moultings from the angels' wings. Neither poet nor painter yet has done full justice to it. Shelley, it is true, has written of the cloud:

> "From cape to cape, with a bridge-like shape,
>   Over a torrent sea,
>   Sunbeam-proof, I hang like a roof;
>   The mountains its columns be."

But his cloud, like everything he touched, was a thing of magnificence and wonder. The quiet everyday effects of light and shade, the dove and dun of a wet December afternoon, the rose and grey of a frosty sunset, all await their poet . . .

One day last week, as I passed on my way to the village, I stopped to watch the hedger-and-ditcher at work. Upon one side of him the thorn boughs lay prone in the puddles; upon the other, the old hedgerow still stood brown and shaggy and berried, just as it *has* stood untouched for a generation or more. I could not help admiring his dexterity as he stripped the shoots which his billhook had spared, drew them down and laid them horizontally, interlacing them to form a long, low fence, about the height and thickness of a hurdle.

"Takes some doin', that does!" he remarked in answer to my unspoken thought.

He was a stranger to Peverel, a tall old man, apple-cheeked and direct of eye, one who knew his own worth, probably, and demanded his due, always taking care to give good value for it. The very way he handled his billhook proclaimed him highly skilled, as, indeed, he must have been, or he would not have been imported to do that especial job while many younger men went workless.

"More rain," he agreed politely, as he drew off his leather gauntlets and beat his arms upon his breast for warmth. "More rain. Yes, and more after that; we're in for a regular spell of it! How do I tell? By th' wind and skies? No. I do not. Not but what they're tolerable harbingers. But I carries my weather-glass about with me. It's just here, in my right shoulder blade, look you; and it's been callin' '*Rain! Rain!*' all mornin', like a young lamb a-bleatin'!"

"Rheumatism?" I suggested, putting all the sympathy I could into the word.

"That's it! Regular Devil's joke of a complaint! Only good thing can be said of it, you knows when to leave your topcoat at home and when to bring it along, for it lets you know when rain's agog twenty-four hours beforehand!"

Every time I have passed since I have stopped for an exchange of weather prophecy. To-day, as he laid the last "quick" and packed up his tools, he confided to me the story of the origin of the complaint he appears to take such a melancholy pride in.

" 'Twas one bitter cold winter back in th' nineties, when th' snow lay on the ground and froze and thawed and froze again, so's it's never been known to do in these parts before nor since. Sheep got buried on th' downs; carts stuck in snowdrifts. Hedges, ditches, fields and everything wer' under snow. All seemed at a standstill!

"Mine was more of a *lay*still than a standstill, though, for right at the very beginnin' I went putting myself forward to help dig some cattle out of a yard, which was none o' my business at all by good rights, and got a chill in my limbs, which turned to rheumatic fever and laid me by the heels for six mortal weeks.

"There I lay and bleated, day after day, with th' pain; and, not bein' exactly a Job by nature, soon got about sick of it. The only thing I had to look forward to was when, at night-time, one or other of th' chaps'd look in and tell me what was doin', or maybe read me a bit out of th' newspaper.

"Very good readin' there was in 'em, too, that winter; for there was a General Election on go, same as there has been this 'un. Only people seemed to get more worked up about it then, for th' workin' man hadn't long had a vote, and he thought, poor chap, it wer' goin' to do wonders! Besides, in our parts, chaps as had been lads at school at the last 'un had grown up, and they wer' beginnin' to read th' papers and think for themselves, puttin' two and two together and makin' four; not takin' their ideas, spoon-fed, from parson and squire, same as their fathers had done before 'em. Another thing, there'd been new cottages built and a paper-mill started, makin' work, so that a good many of 'em didn't even live on the estate, much less work on it.

"Yes. Old Sir Owen, Squire, as he liked to be called, because his forefathers had been squires long before they were baronets. he wer' our member. Every man jack in th' place wer' expected to vote for him; there'd 'a' been the deuce to pay if they hadn't and he'd known it, and when a man owns the very roof over your head where are you if you offend him?

"Well, as I say, things had shifted a bit that time. Some lawyer chap who was opposing Squire came down and talked to th' lads of an evening. Decent sort of fellow he was, too, treated anybody as though they wer' the same sort of flesh and blood as himself, and seemed to know altogether where the shoe pinched with fifteen bob a week and a family to bring up. 'Right's right, and wrong's no man's right!' was his motto; the chaps used to call it out to each other as they passed in the lanes or across the fields as they worked.

"As to me, I liked to hear all and say nothin', and was not sorry on th' whole that I was laid low and couldn't get to th' pollin' booth. Squire's tenant as I was, I couldn't *afford* much of a conscience.

"Well, two days before polling day down comes my lady, Squire's wife that was. I had just dragged myself from the bed to th' chair by th' hearth while bed was made, when in comes she.

"'You'll vote for Squire,' she says, just puttin' her head inside the door, and startin' writin' me off in her little book before I'd a chance to answer.

"'Beggin' your pardon, my lady,' says I, 'but I can scarce crawl from bed to chair, let alone the three miles to th' schoolroom.'

"'Oh, but we'll send th' carriage for you. You'll manage nicely, I'm sure. Where there's a will there's a way, you know!' and she clicked her great teeth together in what she called a smile, as though that bit th' matter off and ended it.

"My missis came in then and began to beg and pray of her. To go out in that bitter raw thaw and fog, she told her, would kill me. But all to no issue. She wer' determined I should go. 'Every vote makes one more,' she said. 'Besides, there is such a thing as duty!'

"Well, on pollin' day, down comes th' carriage at ten o'clock, with two strappin' men-servants on th' box, and I was hauled out of bed, dressed, and driven off before I could say knife. Well, they shoved me about, here, there and everywhere. Had to, for I was like nothin' but a sausage with th' stuffin' out. Glad enough I was to get back between th' blankets again. I shall always say th' hot flat-irons th' missis had put to warm 'em saved my life for me that time.

"No. I lived to vote again, although not without a little keepsake in th' way of that weather-glass in my shoulder; but Squire, he didn't live to stand again, for when he found that th' lawyer chap'd got in he took to his bed and never got up again. Yes, lawyer chap got in, but by a narrow shave; 'twas th' talk of th' country that time, for when all th' countin' and doin' was over they found there was a majority of *one*!"

"So they gained very little by dragging you out through the snow!"

"*Very* little! Terrible little, *indeed!* But t'other chap gained his majority!"...

The gull, which used to be only an occasional visitor, said to fly inland upon the approach of a storm, is becoming almost as much at home here as the rook. It is a common sight all the winter to see gulls stalking up and down the ploughed land, or hovering over the marshes. Towards evening they may be seen winging in twos and three across the heath and over the hills seaward; then the rooks depart in a noisy company, and the twilight sky is left to the plovers, with their melancholy, long-drawn "Peewit!"

From the hawthorn clump upon the heath to-day came the harsh "Chack! Chack!" of the fieldfare. That sound is one of the voices of winter here. From

November until the end of February they fly in bands of ten or twelve, clearing the hedges of the last berries, and, when those fail them, taking to the less palatable holly. They have only been back from their native Norway a week, but already the crimson wash of haws upon the smoke grey of the thorns is thinning, for they have tremendous appetites, and, after they have made a meal upon a tree the earth beneath is strewn with stones and husks.

We, who only know the fieldfare as a winter visitor, are not disposed to count him as a songbird, for no bird we know has a more harsh and grating note; but in his native land he ranks much as the missel thrush does with us, and his song during the breeding season is said to be wildly musical. He shows his cousinship to the thrushes, too, in his speckled breast and full dark eye; but his nature is wilder and shyer. Not even in the most icebound weather will he come to the garden as the thrushes do, but keeps altogether aloof from man.

When our southern winters are too severe for him, he migrates still farther, crossing the Channel for the rest of the winter, and paying us a flying visit upon his way back to the North of Europe in the spring...

The fox has few friends. The farmer detests him for his depredations amongst the poultry; the gamekeeper for his poaching propensities. Even his seeming friends, the fox-hunters, only champion his cause to hunt him to death at the end.

While daylight lasts, he keeps well out of sight, and no wonder, for, should hunger drive him to show himself by day, every living thing he meets is his enemy. Let him but hide himself behind a hedge and every little bird turns informer. Jays, mistle-thrushes, wrens and chaffinches all make common cause and chatter and scream excitedly; even the shrike leaves off beetle-hunting to join in the hue and cry, and the fine fat rabbit Reynard is stalking disappears with a flash of white tail into some convenient burrow.

There are other and even wilder creatures abroad in winter. Sometimes in the dusk of a December day the lingerer in the woods may sight a badger,

stumping upon its short legs across some open space and grunting like a small pig as it goes. Its stumpy appearance, caused by its short, stout legs and general resemblance to the bear, have gained for it in some districts the name of the British bear; but it does not belong to the bear family, being more akin to the otter. In many parts of the country the badger has disappeared entirely; in the woods and about the wilder heaths of Sussex and Surrey there are still a few left, but, as man advances, this fierce, wild denizen of the wilderness retreats, and many people who have spent their whole lives in the country have never seen one.

The otter is a little less rare. Not far from Peverel runs the river Wey,* quite a small stream, early in its career, but fringed with inaccessible marshy thickets, and embracing many small islands in its windings. These are the otter's fastnesses; amongst the underwood and water-weeds it makes its burrow or "holt", only coming out to fish in the stream, or to seize some tempting duck, rabbit, or rat when opportunity occurs. Those who frequent the river banks may now and then catch sight of a dark, flat head, much like the

---

*The river Wey passes north of Liphook, a mile from Weaver's Down.

head of a seal, bobbing above the water as its owner swims from bank to bank. If the observer can manage to remain unseen and unheard, the otter will often mount the river bank and amble about among the meadow-sweet and rushes; or it may even come out on the open green and cross the meadow from one stream to another, for, although its feet are webbed, it is able to move on land with ease . . .

Some time during last night, the wind veered round, and the leaden skies and mild wet winds of yesterday gave place to white frost and white fog. The transformation was complete. The outlines of the woods and hills, lately so dark and clear, were muffled in the woolly whiteness of the atmosphere; through the fog the sun loomed, a dull red disc; rags of rosy cloud showed through the shifting vapour, and the air had the raw, throaty edge of December upon it.

Against the vague whiteness, the garden trees stood plume-like, every branch and twig feathered with frost spicules; only the holly by the gate burned through, scarlet and glossy green, every prickly leaf outlined with filigree.

At seven o'clock, in the strange hush of the frosty morning twilight, a fox trotting home from his nocturnal prowling, passed close by the garden hedge. Evidently, he had lost his bearings in the fog, for the scent of wood-smoke from the cottage chimney threw him suddenly back upon his haunches, and, after one wild, furry scramble, he fled at full stretch across the heath.

No other living creature was in sight. For an hour beyond their usual time, the birds, deceived by the gloom, or discouraged by the cold, lurked discon-solately in the frosted bushes. There is nothing, excepting snow, the small birds dislike more than hoarfrost, heavy rain is bad enough, severe cold worse, but the hoarfrost combines for them the discomforts of both, for the light particles fall from the bushes and powder them unobserved, then, slowly melting, penetrate to the skin, and chill them miserably . . .

Far away, over a small green valley among the heather, a kestrel hung suspended – a small, dark, hammer-shaped speck against a piled-up bank of white cloud. Although at some distance, its presence was at once perceptible in a speedy clearance of the air and a subdued but excited twittering among the bushes. For a few seconds the hawk hung, a figure of dread, then, as though disgusted by the apparent lifelessness beneath it, rose into the upper air with staccato wing-beatings and sailed away over the hills.

Bird of prey as it is, there is yet something pathetic about the solitary figure of a hawk in the sky. Always alone – for it only consorts with its own kind in the breeding season, and wherever it goes the sky is cleared of other birds as though by magic – always friendless, always solitary, it is a kind of Ishmael among winged things.

So it spends the winter, drawing heath after heath and field after field, sinking like a stone at intervals to capture and devour its prey, seldom haunting one locality for more than a day at a time, and roosting at night at whatever point that day's wanderings have brought it to at dusk.

Although the small birds are ter-rified at the sight of anything in the shape of a hawk, and fly before a kestrel as they would before a pereg-rine falcon, birds actually form a small proportion of the kestrel's game-bag. More often it is content to make a meal on a frog or a mouse; while large insects, such as beetles, caterpillars, or even the scaly, unsubstantial gras-shopper, are not disdained.

Although the kestrel is so much more numerous and widely distri-buted than any other of our native hawks that it is the only one known by sight to many people, it is probable that far more havoc is worked among bird life every year by the more murderous though less noticeable sparrow-hawk.

Instead of hovering in the air as the kestrel does, the sparrow-hawk hunts close to earth; sweeping across fields and along hedgerows, dashing through gateways and gaps, it sweeps the crouching, trembling little bird from the twig, or the young rabbit or partridge from the turf, and carries it off without any perceptible pause in its dread career. Even the presence of man has little effect upon this bold freebooter, for it will dash out from behind a rick or byre to snatch up a chick from under the very feet of the farmer's wife as she feeds her fowls . . .

Within the pinewood was a different atmosphere to that of the open heath – shelter instead of sun-warmth; dim blue vistas for sunlight, and, in exchange for the cheerful twittering of birds, the whispering hush of the evergreen pine-tops. Upon the brown earth and scrubby underwood between the long aisles of closely planted trunks scarce a trace of the morning's frost was evident; only the fallen cones, close and small with the damp, showed that the weather had penetrated that thick, evergreen roof.

The footstep fell upon the thick layers of pine-needles without a sound. All was dark, sheltered, and silent, excepting when a jay flashed past with its long, harsh scream, or the wood-pigeons rose with loud wing-clappings above the tree-tops.

Far from the haunts of man; out of the world, as it were, and almost out of the weather, the whole place seemed made for repose. High banks and thick hedges shut out intruders, besides furnishing all manner of nooks and crannies for sleep; the very bushes, each with its drift of dead leaves piled around like walls, were like tiny houses, inviting tenants.

And no doubt, if one had X-ray eyes, almost every likely nook would be seen to be occupied, for to such sheltered and sequestered spots all manner of creatures repair – squirrels from the beech woods; dormice and hedgehogs from the hedgerows; snakes and lizards from the heath – all gathering together in one great dormitory for their winter sleep.

In the layers of dry pine-needles which carpet the earth thousands of insects lie up for the winter, not necessarily to sleep, but with lives narrowed down to the circumference of the stone or slip of dry bark they have crept under. If but a fragment of dead wood is raised whole communities are exposed to view. Ants and earwigs rush here and there; centipedes scramble over each others' backs in their haste to be gone, while the bolder beetles strike quite a militant attitude and butt and spar at the piece of twig thrust gently among them.

It is a striking reflection that each one of these tiny creatures, many of them only known by name to a few entomologists, has its own life to live and its own wonderfully developed manner of living. One of the commonest of the lesser known of these under stone or wood hiding insects is the little brown lithobius, or thirty legs.

So accustomed is it to the darkness of its hidden retreat that its numerous pairs of eyes have become dim for want of use, and it finds its way and searches for its food by means of the two long, highly sensitive feelers upon its forehead. Yet it has its own domestic problems to deal with. The mother lithobius, for instance, has not only outside dangers, but also the cannibal tendencies of her mate to contend against, and, lest he should devour it, she wets her newly laid egg and rolls it in earth to disguise it.

But not only such generally unconsidered atoms of life as the lithobius repay observation; the more we study the most familiar insects, the more we find to admire. The common earwig, for instance, is only *too* well known to most of us, especially to those who take a special pride in their dahlia beds; yet few who know it well as a rather dingy and unattractive looking insect are aware that, neatly folded beneath its scaley brown coat, it carries a most fairy-like pair of wings.

When unfolded for one of the insect's rare flights, these wings flash out, as glistening and delicately veined as those of the much-admired dragon-fly – so beautifully wrought and exquisitely finished, in fact, that one can only marvel that so much beauty should have been created to remain so long unseen . . .

Upon the edge of the heath, by the roadside, a number of Gypsy caravans have drawn up for the winter. Altogether, there must be nearly a score of them, making quite a small town, where women cook, wash clothes, and bath their babies out of doors, calling shrilly the while to the elder children, who, apparently exempt from school attendance, range the heath to gather sticks, or dabble their bare purple feet in the icy pools . . .

The plot they have taken up their winter quarters upon has a curious history. A few years ago, when a large military camp was established a few miles from Peverel, a London business man conceived the idea of buying up all the privately owned part of the heath and founding a kind of garden city.

Roads were marked out and named on maps, and the place and scheme were widely advertised. A few people, tempted by the scenery and good air, built weekend or summer cottages, but nothing came of it.

The garden city never materialised, but the originator of the scheme was not discouraged. Such large undertakings, he said, took time. The public must in time discover this "English Switzerland within forty miles of London", and, when that time came, there would be what he called "a boom". So, to further his plans, he built himself a wooden bungalow upon the spot, labelled it "Estate Office", and took up his residence there.

I do not know what he was like when he came, but I saw him twenty years later, still living alone there, a strange, wild-looking man, unshaven and practically in rags, but still ready to surprise the listener with his cultured accent as he pointed out such and such a heather-covered waste as "Cavendish Square", or recommended another as a "fine corner site".

The spot where he lived himself, and where the Gypsies are now, was to have been the site of a magnificent hotel. He saw it all to the day of his death, a rose-red pleasure city blushing among pines between the North Downs and the seaward hills. "When the war is over," he used to say, "you will see what will happen!"

Upon the raised square of turf which marks the foundations of his long-demolished hut the Gypsies to-day had piled their harvest of berried holly. A fitter memorial, perhaps, for one who loved the heath than the Grand Hotel of his dreams would have been.

INDEX

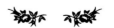

A Note on the Illustrations

With the exception of the map on page 6, which is by Andrew Farmer, all the illustrations in this book are by Charles Tunnicliffe, R.A. (1901-1979), and are taken from the books in which they originally appeared. Acknowledgement is made to the Trustees of the Estate of C.F. Tunnicliffe for permission to reproduce them here.

The books in which they were first published are as follows: Mary Priestley, *A Book of Birds* (1937); Norman Ellison, *Adventuring with Nomad* (1950); Alison Uttley, *Ambush of Young Days* (1951); C.F. Tunnicliffe, *Bird Portraiture* (1945); Sidney Rogerson, *Both Sides of the Road* (1949); Alison Uttley, *Country Hoard* (1943); Arthur Cadman, *Dawn, Dusk and Deer* (1966); Charles S. Bayne, *Exploring England* (1944); Alison Uttley, *Here's a New Day* (1956); H.E. Bates, *In the Heart of the Country* (1942); C.F. Tunnicliffe, *My Country Book* (1942); H.E. Bates, *O More than Happy Countryman* (1943); Henry Williamson, *Peregrine's Saga* (1934); Alison Uttley, *Plowmen's Clocks* (1952); E.L. Grant Watson, *Profitable Wonders* (1949); Norman Ellison, *Roving with Nomad* (1949); C.F. Tunnicliffe, *Shorelands Summer Diary* (1952); E.L. Grant Watson, *The Leaves Return* (1947); Ian Niall, *The Way of a Countryman* (1965); Alison Uttley, *The Country Child* (1945); E.L. Grant Watson, *Walking with Fancy* (1943); Richard Jefferies, *Wild Life in a Southern County* (1949).